W9-CAG-844

THE STORY OF THE
SAILING SHIP

Rosemary and Colin Mudie

Exeter Books

NEW YORK

Copyright © 1975, 1980 Marshall Cavendish Limited
Published in the United States of America
by Exeter Books

First printing 1975
Second printing 1980

Distributed by Bookthrift Inc.
New York, New York 10018

All rights reserved

ISBN 0–89673–057–3

Printed in Singapore

Introduction

The story of the sailing ship is the story of the ingenuity, bravery and curiosity of man. In this age of the jumbo jet and space exploration, it is easy to forget the remarkable courage of those who set sail in wooden ships, without maps or sophisticated navigational instruments and with only the capricious winds and their own skill to propel them. But it is to the designers, boatbuilders and sailors of the past, that we owe our knowledge of the world, its oceans and lands.

From the earliest known civilizations, of Egypt, Greece, Mesopotamia and Scandinavia, we have evidence of man's use of sail propulsion. The sailing ship has changed and developed, become larger or smaller, more powerful and less cumbersome; it has been equipped for voyages of trade and exploration, war and colonization. The rig has been elaborate at the whim of kings and practical for use on every ocean, sea and lake. The beginnings of steam may have brought the age of sail to a close but the vessels have remained or been reconstructed and, even today the seamen of the world's navies learn their trade upon these magnificent ships. This book includes all these, plus those craft still in daily use in China, Japan, Peru and the Far East. At all times the story is a thrilling one, of the challenge of the ocean and of how man has met that challenge.

B 1908

Copyright 1909 by Franz

Contents

Chapter I
The beginnings of sail

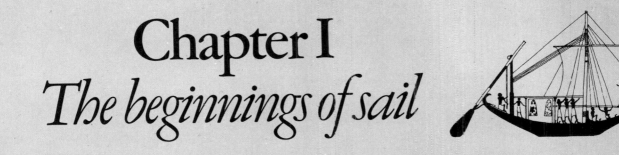

The classic picture of the first man afloat usually takes the form of a bemused looking, fur-clad, apeman inadvertantly adrift on a log. The mirror-like surface of the pond is disturbed only by his hands as he thoughtfully invents paddling. From such a beginning it is tempting to draw a line of research and development through the years, to cover paddling and rowing until we reach man's supreme achievement – sailing to windward.

This of course is evident nonsense. The only mystery about the invention of sailing ships is the quite minor one of record. Sailing in fact is a natural function of anything which floats where a wind blows and that is almost everywhere. The smallest water bug uses the wind to voyage across ponds; leaves, twigs and other items of nature's detritus can do nothing but sail downwind and even the elegant swan is designed to raise a handsome

Below An Egyptian burial boat of about 2040-1780 BC. It was built on the basis of the Dashur boat and would have been contemporary with those found at Saqquara.

Right *A Peruvian papyrus reed boat with full sail. This type of boat is still in use in Peru and until recently was used extensively in Tasmania.*

Below *Fishermen on Lake Titicaca in Peru. The people still use their papyrus reed boats for fishing in the waters of the lake. This type of boat is very similar to those of the early Egyptians. The reeds are bundled together with regular lashings, into a long, thin hull form, in the style of a slight crescent.*

Far right *This buff decorated pot is characteristic of the Nacquara 11, i.e. the Gerzean or pre-Dynastic culture about 3300 B.C. It depicts a sailing boat of that period, with sail and oars. It was probably built of acacia and sycamore, which grow in abundance along the Nile.*

pair of running sails, when the wind serves her purpose. The biggest problem facing the first waterman might well have been how to avoid sailing too smartly away from home and all he held dear. In such a predicament you would find anyone scrabbling in the water with feet and hands, to get back to shore or poking desperately with a stick to stop the craft blowing further and further away. By the time the errant craft had blown clear of soundings, early man would have invented in some form the whole basic gamut of boating right up to the mechanical age in one ten minute span of time.

The real ingredients of development are man and materials. There is little evidence that early man, in historical times at least, was any less intelligent than ourselves. Scarcely educated and less adequately equipped certainly, but no less enterprising and no

By watching the creatures of the water, man discovers Sail

less ingenious than ourselves. Ships and boats represented the front rank of technology for centuries, in fact for all of man's days until the aeroplane. The ship was the space craft of most civilizations and it was designed and built and manned with the same calibre of intellect as nowadays plans voyages among the stars.

The past, dug up from the mud or found in museums or attics, usually looks motheaten, dusty, and worn out. The past as seen in our elders is represented by the tired and aged, giving man a natural feeling of superiority over previous generations and things. It is often difficult for us to visualize early craft when they were new, bright as buttons, clean and smart as yachts and manned by fit and intelligent youngsters.

Our first sailors, therefore, after they got over their baptisms, would quickly realise why they were so rudely propelled over the surface of the sea and no doubt as quickly noticed that they had a fair measure of control over the process. If the wind was fair they could stand up, spread their arms and furs to catch the wind and speed along. If the wind blew the wrong way then it was a question of making a low profile and looking to paddling or stick work to make progress. In no time at all we can see the fur or cloak stuck up on a stick and early man under full sail thinking no more of harnessing nature to help him in this enterprise, than he would about conservation and pollution when drinking from a stream.

Two other practical facts which affect any consideration of the beginning of sailing should also be mentioned. First is that it is not at all easy to get a boat to sail properly down wind. A normal rudderless boat will lie broadside or slightly bows into the wind and drift very slowly, sideways. The downwind boat therefore very often steps the mast well forward to improve the self steering and always will have a rudder or some other means of directional control. The other fact is that the wind seldom blows in a constant direction and therefore any sailor would quickly experience the effects of wind

blowing his craft and sails from every angle. Almost any old rag of a sail in a boat with a rudder will sail it along at right angles to the wind. Early sails, by their very simplicity, were in fact often capable of windward sailing and the only bar to the boat using this capability was the increased sideways drift as the boat is brought up towards the wind. The history and possibility of windward sailing therefore depends very much more on the development of windward working hull forms, than in rig.

Mesopotamia and Egypt, followed by the Mediterranean Sea in general, are usually credited in European civilizations with the beginnings and development of the arts of sailing and voyaging in ships. Possibly Polynesia and the Chinese have equally good claims and by and large it is not a matter of great importance. The real interest lies in the developments in materials and know-how which brought the sailing ship from a log propelled by a fur skirt stuck on a pole, to the more complex scientific miracles of the great days of the clipper ships. Science is not exclusively applicable to test tubes and computers but is equally present in sticks and strings laced together into a pattern of logic and efficiency as beautiful and precise as any printed circuit.

It is thought that the Chinese were using flat rafts made of bamboo at about the time of the beginning of the first stone age, 4000 BC. Another of the earliest civilizations developed between the rivers Tigris and Euphrates and what may be the earliest surviving model sailing boat, dating back to 3500 BC, was dug up there at *Eridu*. It is a high sided, tub shaped vessel with pointed ends and what looks like a mast step inside. One could also believe that the brace across one end might be a helmsman's seat or even a sheet horse for the sail and that the holes in the sides are for shrouds or oars. It is really a bit of a mystery for the hull shape infers that it would most likely be a small craft

Egyptian papyrus fishing canoes, from the tomb of Chancellor Mehenkvetre. In about 2000 BC he was buried with a good collection of models, both of the papyrus boats and of early sailing ships.

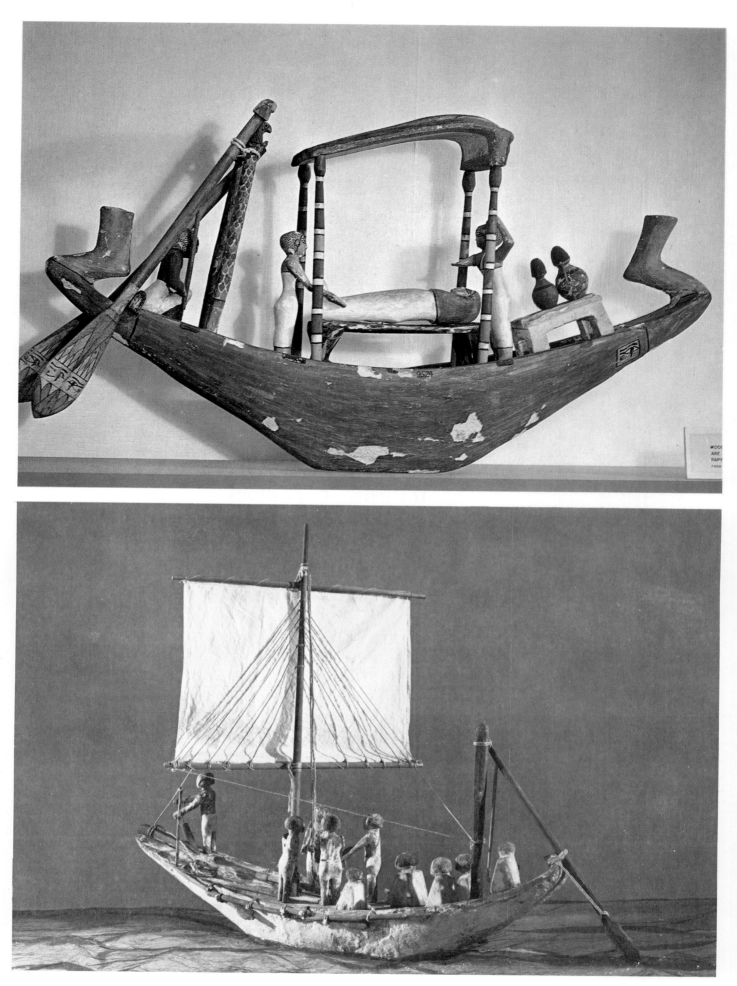

made in a basket type of construction covered with skins whereas the mast step, etc. belong rather more to a bigger vessel which might have been made of wood in a manner not seen again for a thousand years. Another explanation, which may be equally valid is that it is not a model boat at all but a candle holder, fancy dish of some sort, or even an ash tray.

The dynastic periods of Egyptian civilization have left the best traces of their early craft. Before they started, about 3400 BC, with Menes the first Pharaoh it seems likely that the Egyptians were already trading by sea with Syria and Crete, representing offshore voyages of 200 miles or so. However, the principal waterway of Egypt is the River Nile which has normally a good north wind blowing over the north-going current. The Nile boatmen could therefore blow upstream or drift downstream with only the minimum of rowing and the minimum need to develop anything other than straight down wind sailing. Egyptian boatbuilders were not so well served. To hand they had only acacia and sycamore in small trees and a great deal of papyrus reed. It is likely therefore, that the earliest Egyptian boats were essentially spool shaped bundles of reeds, much as are used to the present day in some parts of the upper Nile and in such places as Lake Titicaca in Peru, and even until recently in Tasmania. The reeds were bundled together with regular lashings into a long thin hull form in the style of a slight crescent to lift the ends out of the water. The bundle was made as wide as possible for stability and an extra bundle was put on top so that the crew and cargo rode reasonably dry. One end at least was looped heavily back and secured with stout lashing in the form of a bow string, to give a quite sophisticated method of pre-tensioning the hull against sag when loaded.

Reed vessels, like those of Ancient Egypt are still used in Peru

Thor Heyerdahl in his experiments with seagoing reed rafts, believed that this also allowed a form of articulation to occur when the reed boat was working heavily in heavy seas.

Southern Egyptian archaeologists have found hundreds of pictures of boats drawn it is thought about 2900 BC. These show the typical spool-shaped hulls of reed boats and some show a simple squaresail of apparently modest size, set well forward. These are important as being about the earliest pictures of boats under sail so far discovered. The stem rears up ahead of the sail to a great height with an indication at the top of what may be leads for yard braces and following the same theme there appear to be a pair of outriggers set low on the hull where nowadays one would fit catheads for the bowlines. Both of which, if correctly interpreted, infer that the sail was braced round to suit the wind direction. On the other hand the mast is shown right forward which would indicate a ship used for downwind sailing only.

Reliefs dating from about 2800 BC show workmen in the act of binding up a papyrus boat and also apparently building a boat of wood, and it seems that about this time the Egyptians were becoming skilful in planking hulls from the short planks of the indigenous trees. From models and from excavations of pits made for real ships, Egyptian vessels of this period appear to be about as big as 70 feet in length with a beam of 17 or 18 feet in a wide, flat spoon form. However, the most impressive relics were found in pits close to the pyramid of *Cheops* and dating back to about 2700 BC. A number of vessels were found, all in pieces but excellently preserved. They included the remains of at least one complete ship, dismantled but placed ready for reconstruction, and this is now being rebuilt. She is 140 feet long and has a beam of nearly 20 feet and is said to be both graceful and sturdy. The keel-less bottom

The tombs of Egypt reveal the secrets of Egyptian sailing ships

planking starts with three cedar boards about 6 inches thick down the centre, with other boards edge fastened to them with acacia treenails (wood pegs) glued into place. In addition, the planks are lashed together inside through holes drilled in them, using ropes of halfa grass and then are caulked with papyrus. The shell appears to be further reinforced with some interior frames added after completion of the hull. The timber is Lebanon cedar and the two largest parts are over 80 feet long and nearly 30 inches square. These are longitudinal stiffeners fitted under the deck near to the sides of the vessel.

Cedar was very important to the Egyptians as a boat building material and hieroglyphics show that in 2650 BC Pharaoh Snefru sent no less than forty ships to Byblos to buy cedar. Reliefs dating from 2550 BC show an expedition which Pharaoh Sahure sent to Syria and these show very much the same kind of ships. Built from relatively short blocks of timber, without any real keel, the ships were braced and secured with rope lashings very much of the same style that was used for the papyrus reed boats. The hull was girdled with one or more stout ropes and was further braced in the bowstring manner with a stout rope truss in effect knotted around each end of the hull and braced off the deck on fork-ended poles. These ships had high stem and stern posts but these appear to have no real structural significance and may be no more than ancestral styling retained because they made a convenient leaning post for the lookouts and for decoration.

The sailing equipment was quite interesting consisting of a bipod mast with an apparently tall squaresail set on a yard at the top and probably loose footed at the bottom. The mast is very well equipped with backstays but with only a single forestay, indicating that it normally worked with the wind aft. A feature of most Egyptian ships is the multiplicity of steering oars and in this case three are shown, possibly to be matched by three on the other side of the stern. The alternative method of propulsion is shown as oars which have taken over from paddles with the size of the craft to be propelled.

Left A wooden model of an ancient Egyptian funerary boat, found at Thebes. The shape of the ship, with its two pointed ends rising out of the water, is derived from boats made of papyrus reeds.

Left This Egyptian model of about 2000 BC shows in more detail the rigging and steering mechanisms of these early sailing ships. These models and remains found in other parts of the world give us a fairly clear picture of the chronological order of the development of the sailing ship.

13

The Cairo Museum has two actual boats of the XII dynasty about 2000 BC and others have been excavated at Saqqara. It was part of the beliefs of the time that a boat was necessary to transport the dead on their first trip and therefore boats were buried as a normal part of tomb furniture. The Saqqara boats, it is thought, were actually used to transport the dead across the Nile. One of the boats is about 33 feet long with about 8 feet beam. It is constructed, like the other Egyptian style of ships, without a constructional keel but with a line of carefully fitted centreline planks to which small wood blocks are pinned to complete the planking. Deck beams are fitted projecting through the side planking and secured with a heavy top strake.

A fine collection of model ships was found in Mehenkvetre's tomb

Pharaoh Mentuhotep, who reigned about 2000 BC, had a chancellor called Mehenkvetre who was buried with a good collection of models. One shows a rather refined version of the papyrus boat with the bow and stern covered with a fine decorative leather cover and a painted washboard fitted each side of the centrebody. More interesting perhaps are the models of sailing ships. One of these shows a pole mast counterweighted with a stone to allow it to be raised and dropped with ease. Both the sailing models had the masts just forward of amidships fitted with a wide squaresail. The yard at the top is fitted with three lifts a side while the lower yard at the foot of the sail is similarly supported with even more lifts. The mast is braced against stern winds by a number of stays while there is only a single stay taken forward to a little bowsprit. This would seem to indicate a quite light rig again, not intended for use except down wind in anything other than very light airs. The steering is also interesting for a single steering oar is shown lashed to the stern on the centreline making it the first known rudder. The steering oar was also supported by a lashing to a small vertical post like a mizzen mast, leaving it free to be turned as required by a vertical tiller by the helmsman. The steering oar or oars which were then more normal can be used to paddle or part row a boat round to help her into a new and required course. The fitting of a fixed centreline rudder indicates either that the boat was unusually handy or, more likely, that she normally used her rowing crew for any great manoeuvring.

In 1480 BC in the XVIII dynasty, Queen Hatshepsut organised an expedition to Punt (thought to be somewhere in Somaliland) and the

This Egyptian fresco shows one of the boats of Queen Hatshepsut's journey to Punt. The event was recorded with some fine reliefs and frescos in 1480 BC. These ships seem to be a little more advanced and may have been constructed with some kind of keel, perhaps similar to those of East Africa and the Indian ocean today. This fresco, discovered at Deir-el-Bahari, shows details of the ship, with deck beams and more complex sail and rigging.

15

Below *These drawings are from the expedition of Karl Richard Lepsius in 1842-45. The journey was from the Sudan to Syria. The ships returned with an extensive collection of casts, drawings and original antiquities and papyrii. Pictures 2 and 3 dated 2040-1780 BC. 1, 4, 5, 6, 1567-1080.*

event was recorded with some fine and detailed reliefs which have been found at *Thebes*. The ships look a little more advanced and may indeed be constructed with some kind of keel following perhaps the current practice in the Indian ocean ships or the East African ships. Those shown are about 70 feet in length with a beam of about 18 feet and a depth of about 5 feet. In addition to a keel they appear to be fitted with deck beams projecting through the shipside and secured with a heavy sheer strake. The deck beams may be fitted to support the deck only but it is likely that they were fitted primarily to brace the topside construction in

addition to the heavy rope supports fitted in the then normal manner. The wide shallow squaresail is supported by a single pole mast with both fore-stays and backstays but still without shrouds. The upper and lower yards of the squaresail are each built from two spars lashed together and extensively supported by lifts. Although the upper yard only is shown fitted with braces for controlling the direction

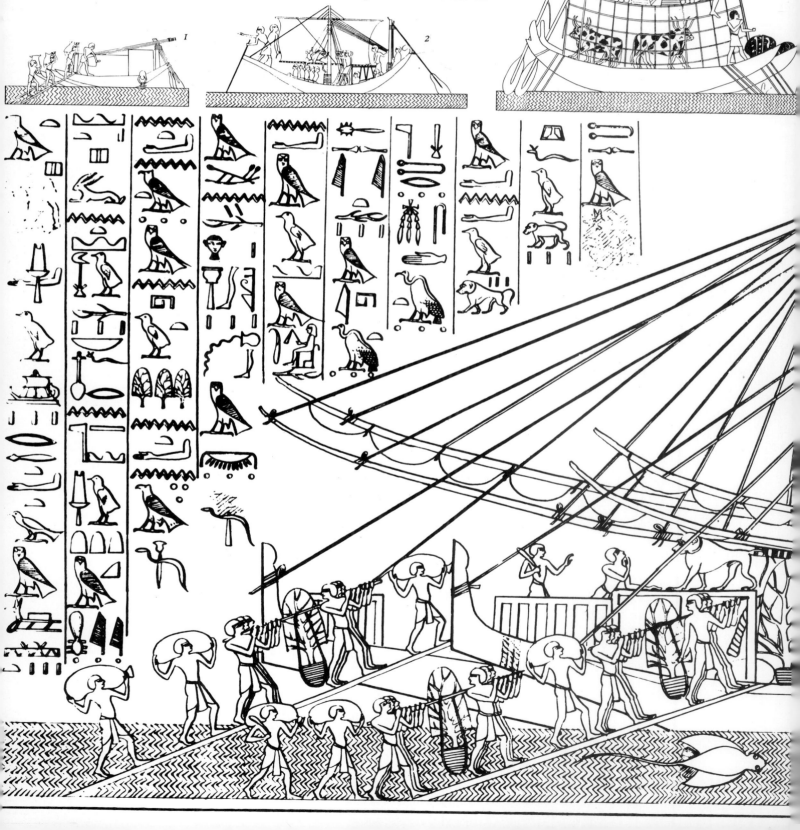

of the sail and no shrouds are fitted, the whole craft appears to be much more of a seagoing type. The spars look heavier and fenced platforms are fitted to both bow and stern.

Queen Hatshepsut also had ships built to carry large stone obelisks and it seems quite remarkable that these were no less than 195 feet in length and 70 feet in beam.

The model sailing ships recovered from the tomb of Tutenkhaman are rigged very much as those shown of the Punt expedition but with one small useful improvement. The steering oars are now carried by a transverse beam, a method which persisted right through Greek and Roman times until the steering oar was superceded by the rudder as we know it.

It is in the nature of man to fight and therefore it must have been as normal to fight your enemies afloat as it was to attack them on land. It is surprising therefore that the first representation of an actual sea battle is to be found in the tomb of Ramses III at *Medinet Habu* dating from about 1200 BC. These are actual warships for they have tops at the mastheads – little basket type platforms were fighting men could shower down the appropriate types of death and destruction on the enemy. As significant

Bottom This illustration shows a further stage in the expedition to Punt. It shows the crew taking on board a cargo of incense and trees. The ships were constructed to carry much greater and heavier cargoes than previous discoveries would suggest had been attempted before.

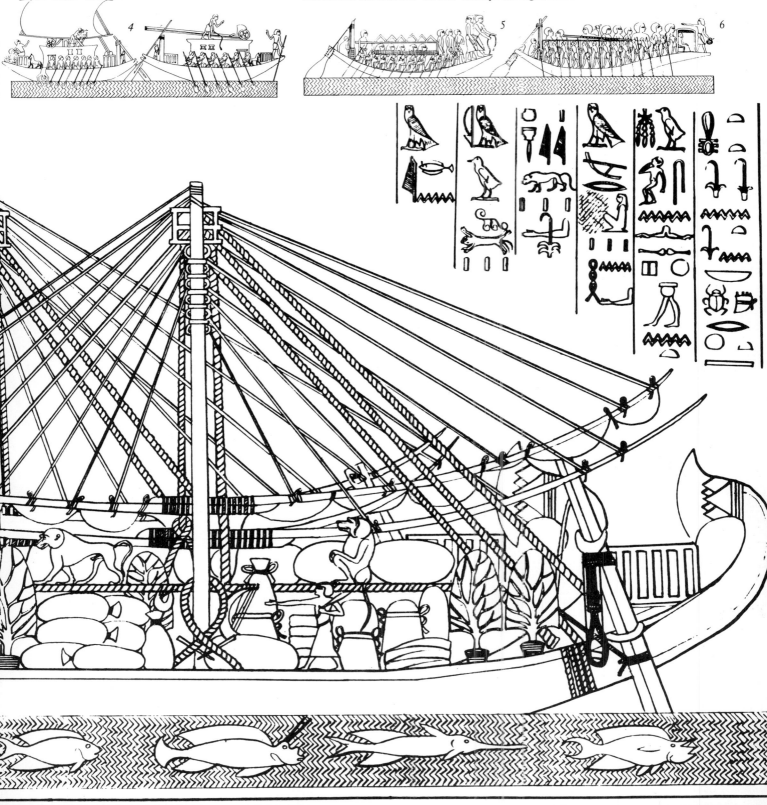

both for general seafaring and for sea wars the sails are fitted with a system of brails. These are a system of lines whereby the sail is furled to the yard which is then left aloft. The ship could therefore press into battle at full speed and then reduce sail without cluttering up the deck which was presumably packed with soldiers. This innovation is thought to have come from the northern Mediterranean and is part of the whole invention of the reefing sail. In fact the sail developed about this time with reefing lines to the yard at its head and a free foot became the universal sail of the Greeks and Romans.

The main line of sailing ship development then seems to have swung away from Egypt and to the

Greeks and Romans. In fact, a description by Herodotus in 400 BC of Egyptian trading craft speaks of vessels built of blocks of acacia as one would build a wall, caulked with papyrus, and pinned together with wooden pegs and all without ribs. An account which would have been valid a thousand years or more before.

This Egyptian fresco, from the tomb of Nakht, was discovered at Thebes and depicts further examples of the advances in boat building.

FARNACES
MAGISTER

ARA

CANTVS

Chapter II
The mediterranean ships

By the second century BC, the Romans had developed
quite elaborate cargo ships. This picture shows a grain
ship of that period. The developments achieved by the
Romans set the standards in form and equipment
which were to be more or less standard features of ships
in Europe until the Middle Ages.

Above *This clay model boat from Mochles dated about 2500 BC shows a vessel resembling a dugout. It confirms to some degree, the theory that boats of this period were fitted with a vertical sternpost and washboards.*

Right *This Minoan clay seal from Knossos has two signet impressions. A ship with a central mast, and it appears an oar, is shown on the left.*

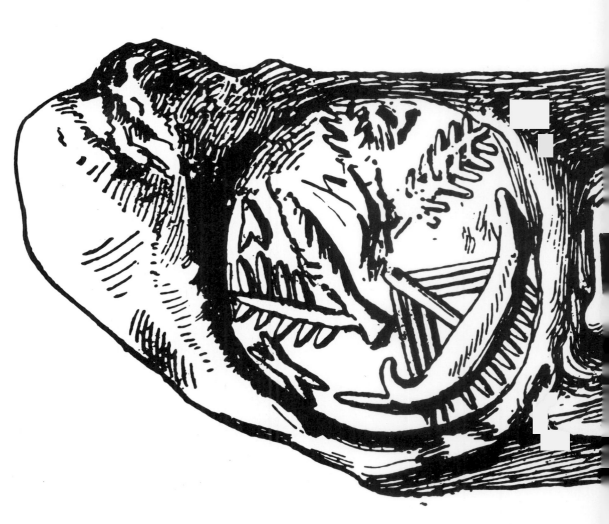

Far left A detail from a relief found at Ninevah Mesopotamia, describing the expedition of King Senacherib to Phoenecia. It depicts a Phoenecian war galley of about 700 BC, powered by rows of oarsmen. These ships had a long pointed prow, set low down which was used to ram and sink boats.

Left The simple dugout canoe, known to date back about 5,000 years, is still in use in many parts of the world today. This picture shows canoes of the lagoon fishermen of Dahomey in West Africa.

The ancient Mediterranean civilizations were undoubtedly strongly influenced by their big and thriving neighbour, Egypt, and probably mostly in the design of their ships, which were the main point of contact between the two. On the other hand their seafaring needs were a little different and above all they had the precious big trees to help them get afloat. It is natural to guess that the first extensive boating might have occurred between the multitude of Aegean islands both for colonising and later for war and for trade. The Mediterranean sea is notorious in the summer months for long periods of very light winds which can whip up quickly into strong winds and rough seas. The sensible boatman would therefore want to make his voyages as quickly as possible in the smooth periods and to get his boat ashore and safely dragged up the beach for the rough. To go further afield than quite local voyages therefore and especially when it was necessary to cross open water the Mediterranean seaman wanted, above everything else, speed. Speed is of course a very great asset for a warship as well. This initial lack of ability to deal with rough weather is also shown by the fact that in ancient times all seafaring more or less came to a stop about October and did not start again until the following April.

It is believed that Aegean trading started or at least was going on as early as 3400 BC, a hundred years before the Dorians drove down into Greece at the start of the iron age. Greek ships of the period were thought to be essentially dug-outs. Pictures on vase fragments dated as 2800 BC show what looks very much like a dug-out fitted with a vertical sternpost and washboards and this is confirmed to some degree by a clay model dug up in *Crete*. Gems and seals show further examples of the type between 2200 and 2000 BC, fitted with a curiously shaped forward post which might be anything from a convenient method of attaching the forward end of the washboards to a full blooded offensive ram. Nowhere, however, is a sail to be seen and pre-

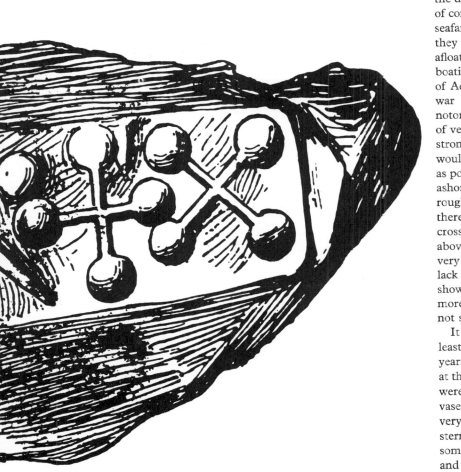

sumably a sail did not make a great deal of sense in a long thin craft normally used in calm weather.

From about 2000 BC onwards, however, it seems likely that sails were used all over the Mediterranean and this more or less coincides with the start of the golden age of the Cretan/Minoan sea trading empire, which flourished until about 1400 BC when the Mycenae invaded from the mainland and destroyed that civilization. Presumably the Minoan ship building craft was not altogether lost but dispersed among surrounding tribes. Cretan gems and seals show pictures of sailing ships with an upper and lower yard square sail very similar to the Egyptian kind. These early pictures appear to show that they

The use of sail coincided with the Golden Age of the Cretan empire

were built with some form of planked construction and indeed this is the basic style of the Mediterranean ship. Probably it developed as an extension of the washboards added to a log or dug-out canoe to keep the crew dry, but it is thought that framed construction with ribs and keels and familiar to modern Europeans was started in the Aegean about 2000 BC. Such a construction, particularly the use of the keel, is often taken as a measure of the advance of boatbuilding methods. It is a little suspect, however, since it must depend heavily on how the ship is to be used in life. A keel on a Nile boat, for instance, would just stop it travelling in shallower water whereas it would be a very desirable feature for a craft which had to be pulled up on the sand every night. Modern boatbuilders are, for instance, just leaving framed and keeled boatbuilding behind for a new construction essentially similar to some of the more archaic processes.

The sails of the period were normally of linen cloths, sewn together (possibly because of the small loom size which restricted the widths available) although the Egyptians sometimes still used papyrus. By 1500 BC the ubiquitous squaresail began normally to be set between two yards or an upper yard and a boom. It is not clear why this was necessary, except perhaps that the generally increasing size of ships and their sails was putting an undue strain on the seaming. It might also have been an attempt to improve performance in light winds by supporting some of the weight of the sail from below, much as is done with a modern spinnaker in the same conditions. Sails were reefed to the lower yard or boom and it is likely that the sail was dropped on the deck for this to be accomplished. With the very wide sails of the period this must have been an extremely awkward manoeuvre and even dangerous as the sail had to be dragged fore and aft to get it onto the deck.

By about 1200 BC the lower yard was discarded

Right Phoenecian ships. This picture shows part of the relief from Konyunjuk, one of the two mounds under which Layard discovered the ruins of Ninevah. The ships are part of the Phoenician navy in which Luli, King of Tyre and Sidon, fled from the Assyrians.

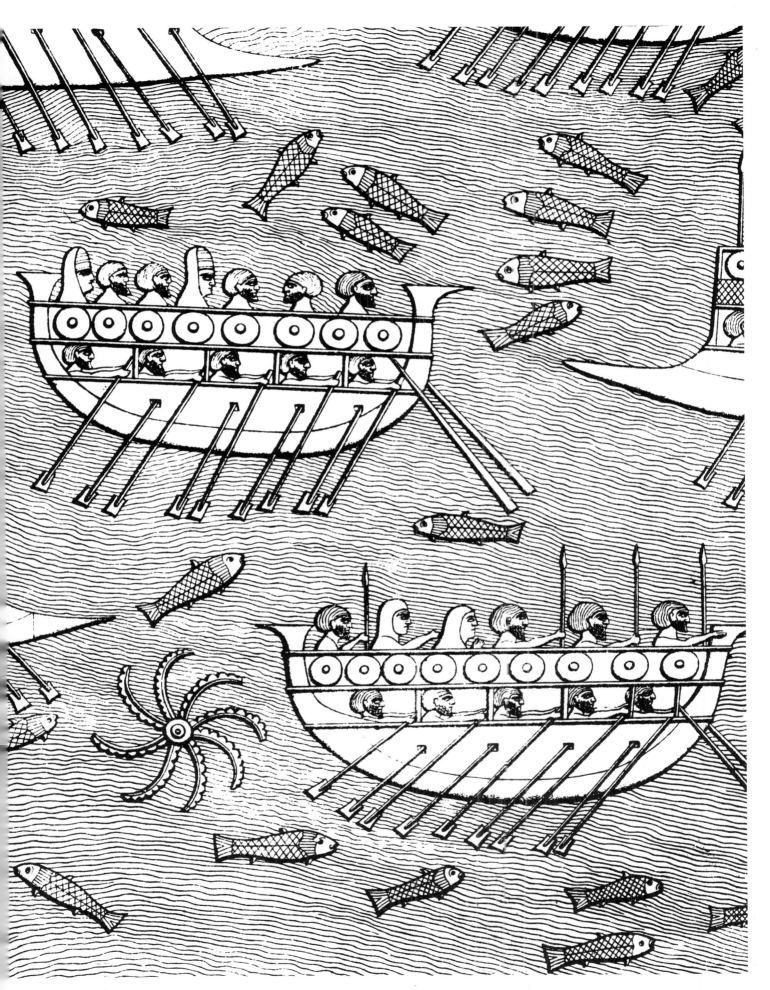

Above This Roman mosaic was found in North Africa. It depicts Ulysses tied to the mast of his ship. His ship and the methods used in its construction, are described by Homer in the Odyessy. It is this work which gives the first real description of Greek ship building of that period.

Left This illustration shows the god Dionysius on his boat, a typical Greek ship of that period. The cup on which the boat is inscribed is by Exekias and is dated about 530 BC.

and the sail fitted with reefing or brailing lines threaded to them so that they could be pulled up to the main yard from lines led down to the deck. This allowed a simple and easy reduction of sail or even its more or less complete removal without involving the cargo or soldiery on the deck, and of course the whole operation could be accomplished at higher speed. This rig became the standard for the Greeks and Romans and in essence persisted to the very last days of the clipper ships. In the Mediterranean it was ultimately eclipsed by the lateen with the spread of the Arab civilization.

From the fall of the Minoans the mainland Greeks became the foremost traders. They held Crete and established colonies all along the trade routes and for five hundred years or more ran the sea lanes from Italy to Syria. There are no real records of what the Greek merchant ships looked like at this time and the nearest picture we have is probably that of the Phoenician ships shown on Kenamon's tomb. It may be the influence of the Egyptian artist, but they look very like the Egyptian ships although the absence of the rope girdling implies that they were probably built of long planks, possibly on frames, rather than with Egyptian wooden 'bricks.' In form they were rather short ended, deep bodied vessels built for capacity rather than speed, the hallmark of the merchant ship of all ages.

The warships of the period started out no doubt as ships which were used for the transport of troops but as warfare and in particular sea raiding or piracy became important they must have developed special characteristics. First among these would have been speed to allow them to overtake their prey and to escape and second would come manoeuvrability. Speed is related to the power/weight ratio and to length and therefore the seagoing pirates would certainly have preferred the much lighter planked vessels than the block construction of the Egyptians. In order to get speed they would be long and thin and filled with as many oarsmen as possible. Manoeuvrability in a long, thin vessel depends very much on the rowing power and this must have added a second spur towards the invention of double banked rowing systems. The first actual picture of a bireme is shown on two Assyrian reliefs from *Ninevah* dated about 700 BC. However, the flourishing time for sea raiding about 1000 BC makes it likely that these vessels were developed earlier to meet an urgent demand. The Mediterranean rowing vessel also usually carried a single squaresail but with such a narrow beam it is unlikely that it was used, except for down wind sailing in lightish winds.

The great enterprise of the sea raiders of Greece was the siege of Troy which is usually dated about 1180 BC and this, through Homer, gives us a fairly

Above The unwieldy Persian galleys could not manoeuvre in the dangerous waters and many ran aground or smashed into one another.

good description of their craft. There appear to have been two main types of ship, a small type about 40 feet in length carrying twenty oarsmen and a larger type possibly 90 feet in length and carrying fifty oarsmen. They were long, thin, light craft renowned for their swiftness and graceful lines and, as 'hollow ships' probably undecked, except for platforms at the ends protected by lattice fencing against enemy spears and the worst of the waves. The mast was unstepped when rowing but with a fair wind would set the classical single loose footed squaresail. The yard is fitted with braces but in most down wind sailing, the most efficiency is given over quite a wide range of wind angles with the sail set square across the ship and so the braces were probably used more for controlling and supporting the wide yard than to adjust it.

Odysseus' famous wanderings on his way home from the siege and sack are described in detail by Homer and include what may be the earliest description of ship building, other than that for Noah's ark. Odysseus had been wrecked and set about building himself a new craft. Fortunately his goddess had fitted him up with an axe, an adze, and a drill, the full tool kit for the boatbuilder of the day. In essence he built a raft of some 20 squared trees in a boat shape, all pinned together with treenails. Then he set up ribs like fenceposts, secured the tops with a rail and added some side planking. It goes on to say that he fenced the hull with lattice bulwarks to keep the water out and heaped brush upon it. It is a complete description of how a boat could be built and leads to the interesting thought that watertightness of the planking would not matter very much. The boat was essentially a raft with a fence around it which would float high. A lining of brush would help both to keep his feet out of any water that swilled over the planking and to dissipate any that came in through the topsides. Over this useful craft it is reported that Odysseus made a fine sail and set it up in the usual fashion. A broad oar to steer with and he was ready for launching.

Only a few years later, about 1100 BC, Jason set off in his 50 oared galley, the *Argo*, on his exploratory voyage to the ends of the Black Sea for the legendary Golden Fleece. Jason and Odysseus, in common with other sea raiders of the time had boats which were crewed by companions and not by slaves. It is usual in these days to confuse galleys with those stories of later times and to think of the oarsmen as slaves suffering under lashes and near starvation. Quite apart from the sheer unlikelihood of anyone treating the power plants on whom life and living depended at sea in this manner the early galleys were manned by a crew of equals. Jason, for example, had in his band many who had been

Left *An alabaster relief from the palace of King Sargon (722–705 BC) at Khorsabad, Assyria. It shows wood being unloaded from Phoenecian ships.*

Overleaf *A Greek merchant ship and a war galley are shown on this Greek vase, dated about 530 BC.*

29

educated with him by his tutor the centaur Cheiron. A place on a raiding ship was probably highly coveted both for the honour and for the booty. In any case when full power was required to run into or away from the battle nothing but a wholehearted team effort would do.

The importance of the voyage of Jason lies in it being one of the first recorded real voyages of exploration by the Mediterranean peoples. From the Aegean he sailed deliberately into unknown waters, through the Bosphorus and Dardanelles to creep all the way along the north coast of the Black Sea to Colchis and their golden fleece. The principal phase of such exploration belongs however to the Phoenicians, probably the greatest sea faring race ever recorded in history. About 1200 to 1100 BC the combination of the decline in Egyptian power and the pressures from the Assyrians behind them, stirred them from their comfortable trading position in the middle of the trade routes. They set off on extensive trading, exploring and colonizing activities which took them right out of the Mediterranean and which were to continue until they were absorbed by the Persians about the sixth century BC. They have left very few records of their ships apart from their contacts with the Egyptians. One of the most important relics is a Phoenician wreck dating from about 1250 BC discovered off *Cape Gelidya* on the coast of Anatolia, Southern Turkey, by Peter Throckmorton. The vessel was excavated by George Bass and proved to be a fairly small ship some 33 feet in length. Of course, very little of the structure of the ship remains. What there is would seem to show a planked construction of cypress on oak. She was carrying a load of copper and may have been the ship of an itinerant smith. It also appears that she did not have a fireplace on board which seems to confirm what common sense would suggest, that such a small ship would look for a beach each night for her cooking and working fires.

Whereas the Phoenicians set up carefully placed trading posts, the Greeks colonized the edges of the Mediterranean in a wholesale manner. Greek trade expanded with them and the Greek trader followed the colonies to Italy, Sicily, North Africa and the Black Sea. A vase found in *Etruria* and dated to about 500 BC shows a Greek merchant ship, a valuable reference since, for some reason or other, the Greek writers who are fairly voluble on other affairs are not very explicit about their cargo ships. It shows a comparatively small ship, some think as small as 30 feet long, although this may be an underestimate, based on the size of the helmsman shown on it. Certainly the amount of rigging shown would have been unnecessary at that size. The hull shape looks as if it follows something of the full, fat form of any trader. At the bow it looks likely that the keel is extended forward to give some additional lateral plane under water and the only purpose for this feature would be to improve the windward sailing capability. The single standard squaresail is shown partly brailed up and she is fitted with a longitudinal gangway over the cargo and a ladder carried aft for climbing off and on the ship when she was beached.

This ladder was as ubiquitous a fitting in those days as is the Mediterranean gangway in modern yachts, using the same area. The stern shows that delightful Greek boatbuilding custom of tying the ends of the longitudinal wales together to end the hull proper but letting them flow on beyond so that they look like the tail feathers of an exotic bird. The principal interest of this picture, however, lies in the illustration of windward ability. Certainly the simple squaresail, rigged in the manner shown, would have quite good, in fact possibly excellent, characteristics for windward work depending mostly on the cut of the sail. The bow extension, sometimes called the cutwater, is of little value downwind and

Below A painting from the buried city of Pompeii depicts a decorated Roman galley. Extensively used for trade, galleys were also formidable warships.

Below A painting from the buried city of Pompeii depicts a decorated Roman galley. Extensively used for trade, galleys were also formidable warships.

Above This relief shows a Roman galley. These ships were used both as warships and as traders within the Empire. This vessel was used for ferrying wine barrels.

Left Mosaics depicting two sailing ships from this period. The mosaics give a good impression of the sails and steering oars of these ships.

Above A Roman grain ship. It was thought that these vessels could carry enough grain in their holds to service a city the size of Athens for a whole year.

Right A third century Roman mosaic, found at Thugga in Tunisia.

Far right Two Roman coins. The one above shows a warship, while the lower coin bears the eagle, a symbol of power.

in fact may tend to increase a tendency for the craft to sheer about. Reaching with the wind abeam or to windward, however, it is a positive improvement with the forward cutwater and the large rudder balancing the sail. No rowers are shown on this illustration and this may not be significant but at this time some windward ability would have been of much greater value to the merchant than to the warship commander. Rowing crew not only have to be fed but they take up valuable cargo space.

Warships developed rapidly to adapt to the rigours of conflict

Further, although it might be possible to plan sailing voyages around the trade routes without windward work (though even this is doubtful) it would certainly have been necessary to work the ship into all manner of ports and anchorages and even to manoeuvre her around when she got there. A further indication of windward ability is the two rudders shown port and starboard. A wide bodied merchantman with the wind abeam or ahead will take up an angle of heel lifting the weather rudder. Two rudders are necessary therefore so that the lee rudder can be used on either tack. Galleys and downwind ships which do not heel unduly, could get by with a single rudder.

The Greeks were not so reticent about their warships and these were invariably what we call these days motor sailers. They were crammed with rowers for speed and fighting and fitted with a small downwind sail which was removed when rowing. The advances in this kind of warship lay principally in the methods of packing in bigger manpower plants and in fitting better fighting platforms for the soldiers and better protection for the rowers. There is a great deal of discussion on how the various banks of rowers were arranged as trireme succeeded bireme and was superseded by quadriremes and quinqueremes. It seems most probable that few ships ever got beyond three actual banks of oars and the mind boggles at the other extreme possibility that five men were working each sweep. Two men to an oar, seems to be the maximum physical possibility one would work efficiently today and therefore it seems likely that the quinqueremes may have run three banks of oars a side, with two of them double banked at full power.

The hull form of the galleys is extremely interesting. The long ram bow was used of course as a weapon, but modern naval architecture would seem to suggest that the long semi-submersible form was also highly desirable for such craft when under way in peace. The long full buoyant form will itself increase the maximum speed at which the hull can travel but in addition sets up a bow wave system which can be out of phase with the main hull waves. A certain amount of cancelling out goes on and the waves set up by the hull when moving can be greatly reduced. Apart from hull efficiency this would make the co-ordination of dozens of closely spaced oars much easier.

The Romans, it is agreed, were not really a sea-

faring race and only took over the Greek seafaring empire and penetrated to the ends of the known world in a somewhat dull manner. Their principal contributions to marine warfare were items of hardware to lock craft together for combat. They also added a forward sail to their warships but one suspects that this advance came from the merchantmen who would find it an aid to manoeuvring in harbour. The principal obsession of the Romans was with the transport of grain about their empire and with its protection. They seem to have developed the craft of shipbuilding particularly in terms of precise workmanship and in sheer size.

A Roman grain ship which put into the port of Piraeus in the second century BC is described by a slightly astonished reporter as being about 180 feet in length with a beam of about 45 feet. Even more astonishing is that her depth was recorded as being about 44 feet in the hold and her capacity enough to keep Athens in grain for a whole year. Lucian, who recorded these details, also mentioned that she had cabins in the stern and, noted for the first time, a topsail, probably set between the masthead and the yard, something like a modern raffee.

The mysterious Nemi ships were excavated at Lago di Nemi

There are many pictures of Roman merchantmen and one can see developing all the details of form and equipment which were to be more or less standard in Europe until the Middle Ages. The hulls were full bodied load carriers, probably with a finer and more raking bow than stern. They were wood planked on close-set frames and also incorporated sets of heavy planks called wales, both to take chafe in the dock and to contain the planks against heavy caulking. The principal cabins are aft and a stern gallery is usually fitted. The mast, still carrying its simple single squaresail, is now heavily fitted with side shrouds in addition to the backstay and forestay arrangement with which the rig started out. She is steered by twin steering oars contained in side galleries and forward there is a high raking bowsprit carrying a small squaresail called an artemon. Some illustrations appear to show twin triangular topsails set over the yard and the stern sports a decorative beakhead or swan head as a last remnant of the Greek bird tail. All in all the Roman merchantman looked a tough and seaworthy craft, intended for winter use in the Mediterranean and also for use outside the Pillars of Hercules into Atlantic waters.

No mention of Roman ships and shipbuilding would be complete without reference to the mysterious *Nemi* ships excavated from *Lago di Nemi* in the mountains above Rome. These superbly constructed vessels were both approximately 240 feet in length although one was 110 feet in beam and the other only 47 feet. How they arrived there or what they were is an unsolved puzzle but one that illustrates more clearly than any picture the skilful state of the boatbuilding art at the time of the Roman empire.

Left A Roman grave slab found at Ravenna in Italy shows a boat builder at work. The slab is from the first century AD.

Below *This illustration shows a model of a typical double ended ship from the early 14th century.*

Chapter III
The northern ships

Of all the primitive civilisations which developed the boat and the sailing ship, that which has made the biggest impact in terms of craftsmanship and seamanship has been that of the Norseman. Scandinavia covers a large area and a large range of climatic conditions, from the more or less treeless north to the prime timber forests of the south. The conditions for seafaring are equally varied, ranging from sheltered fjords to rough open waters of the North Sea. Sea transport was extremely important to most of Scandinavia, as much in the mountainous north as it was among the myriad islands of the Baltic. Even village life depended heavily on the day to day use of the boats and for more extensive voyaging, there was always the North Sea to keep a fine edge on their seaworthiness. Even today the typical Scandinavian boat is fine ended and narrow and with that apparent lack of stability which is appreciated only by the open water sailor who knows that it means an easier ride in rough seas.

The earliest records of Scandinavian boating are rock carvings going as far back as 2000 BC and continuing until about 200 BC. The early carvings show curious wispy looking boats. These are apparently the northern boats built of light branches and covered with leather – the materials of the Eskimos until quite recently. They appear to be built with two main top members which extend out beyond the skin cladding of the boats to form handles. These were probably used to carry light boats bodily up and down to the sea. The bigger and heavier boats show a sort of bottom skid keel also

protecting fore and aft of the skin hull and, forward, arcing upwards. The heavier boats would not be easily lifted and would therefore have to be run up over the rocks. A sledging community would naturally fit something akin to a sledge runner for this purpose. This arrangement could only be guessed at until an actual boat was dug up in the island of *Als* in Denmark showing this style exactly, except for one curious difference. She was planked elaborately in wood planks edge sewn together, in place of the leather covering which would fit this construction method so well. Perhaps it represents, being found so far south, a translation of a satisfactory northern boat into an environment where timber was easier to come by than animal hides.

In the timber country, dugouts were of course the

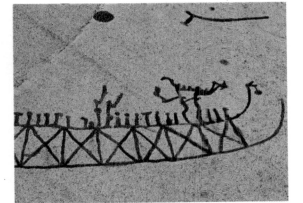

Far Left *A picture stone from Gotland in Sweden shows the eight legged horse of Thor and below a northern sailing ship.*

Left *A Bronze Age drawing of about 1000 BC, from Tanum in Sweden, shows a type of wooden framed, skin covered boat.*

Below *Rock carvings from Bohuslan, Sweden showing early vessels similar to that found at Tanum.*

Below A modern skin-covered eskimo canoe. These boats are still built in the traditional style, a light framework covered with tightly stretched skin.

natural starting boat and thousands have been found all over wooded Scandinavia. They were in fact built until the last century so we are fairly knowledgeable about all the variations which were probably in common use years ago. These include craft which had outriggers like a trimaran and two craft strapped side by side to give better load carrying and stability. Most interesting, however, is the method of softening and spreading the dugout

canoe with applied heat. Ribs were then fastened into this, both to keep the shape which had been achieved and to form a framework on which to secure washboards also sewn to the hull proper. It takes only a very little step from that to add another plank and yet another and arrive at the fully planked clincher built hull which is the masterpiece of the Northman.

The Mediterranean boatbuilder laid his planks one beside the other, when he fastened them to the hull. The Northman overlapped them, securing them through the overlap so that the skin of the ship was basically strong and rigid without additional framing, although this was added for additional strength. It is a construction which requires great skill and good clear straight timber. Scandinavian ships had to be dragged out of the water in the winter months to keep them clear of the ice and this put an extra premium on strong, lightweight constructions.

The next clue we have as to the development of the Northern ships is Tacitus who mentions that in his time, approximately 100 AD, that the Scandinavian vessels, unlike the Roman vessels, were the same at both ends. The first direct evidence, however, was the finding of a big ship dating back to 300 AD in a bog at *Nydam* in Schleswig. This vessel was 75 feet long and nearly 11 feet in beam and showed a direct development from both the dugouts and the skin boats. The planking overlaps and at the ends is allowed to run naturally in a high, sheer curve, another feature of the classical Northman's ship. She is an oddity in her way, because she was built with a centreline keel plank rather than the normal projecting keel. As this would have made her very vulnerable when hauling out, it seems likely that she was a native boat built for the softer conditions of the south. She would normally lie afloat or take the ground on soft mud. This is

Below These coracles, made from skins or tarred canvas stretched over a wicker frame, can still be found on the river Teifi in Wales. The coracle was first used by the ancient Britons.

Right A reproduction of a Viking longboat on a fjord. The longboats were built to glide silently close to the coastline with maximum stealth and speed and were constructed to carry horses as well as fighting men.

Below The interior of the Gokstad ship found preserved in an Oslo fjord. She is about 76 feet long with 16 planks aside and 16 pairs of oars. This ship was thought to be the private karvi of a chief.

partly confirmed by the ton of ballast that was found in her, for this would have been highly unpopular if it has had to be manhandled into her every time she went afloat. Whether the ballast was to make a fast boat more stable, or to correct some problem with the naval architecture, we cannot know.

Another find was that of the two ships at *Kvalsund* from the seventh century. The bigger of the two was about 60 feet long with 10½ feet beam. She has a much flatter bottom than the Nydam ship and is fitted with a deliberate keel for hauling out. The extra stability from the beam would give her a much better sailing performance and sails in fact were commonly shown in drawings of the period. Norse sails would seem to have been made from fairly poor material. At any rate it had to be cross-banded with reinforcements of doublings of material and even possibly leather, to strengthen it sufficiently. This material weakness shows right through the early part of the Viking era. At first the sail, a single squaresail, was set to a lower yard, presumably to spread the load on the bottom seam into what was in effect a timber reinforcement. Later, when the lower yard was abandoned, the bottom edge of the sail was not controlled by the normal sheets and bowlines to the corners but by a multiplicity of sheets all along the bottom edge. Only an urgent

need to spread the strain could have driven a seaman to such a complication. The sails, involving so much hand work anyway, were a natural subject for decoration and must have shown a marvellous sight to the world.

The rig was extremely simple. The relatively short, pole mast which was easily lowered for rowing and camping, was stayed fore and aft, with the sail and its yard pulled up on a halyard which was taken aft to act as an additional stay. The yard was adjusted and controlled by conventional braces and for going to windward with the sail pulled more along the length of the hull, the weather leach of the sail was held out by a wooden spar. Such a rig, in such a hull shape, would certainly reach across the wind well enough and the windward performance was probably more limited by the bagginess of the sail than anything else. It seems likely that some boats of the period sported cutwaters in the Mediterranean style, but this may be more of a method of supporting the stem from an extended keel than a specific intention to improve the windward ability. A single rudder was carried on the starboard side as the steerboard side became known. Many steering positions are developed in relation to prevailing winds and so forth, but it seems most likely that the steering oar in Northern ships was

Above *The 7th century ship found at Kvalsund.*

Above *The early Norse vessel found at Als.*

Above *The Nydam ship, first example of a Norse ship.*

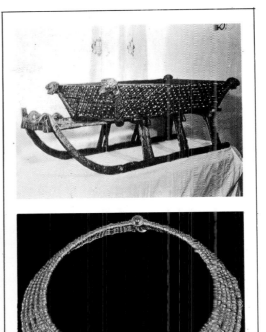

Left *These Norse treasures were found in the wreck of a longboat, possibly a funeral vessel.*

Opposite and below *These are two views of the Gokstad ship, one of the very best examples of a Viking vessel to be excavated. She was named after the Oslo fjord where she was found.*

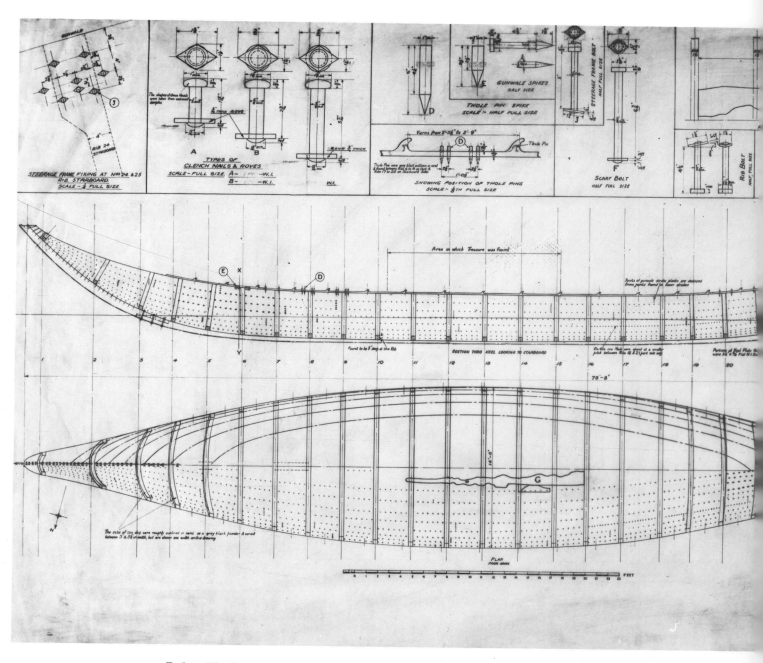

Below The Sutton Hoo vessel shown in cross section, from the excavated remains.

Above The Sutton Hoo vessel, dating from about 650 AD. This plan and the photographs below show the clench nails used in her construction.

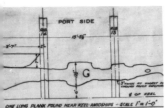

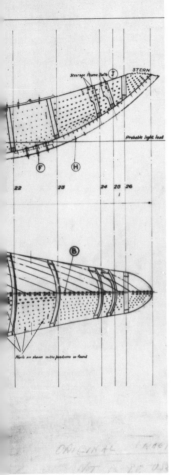

placed there, only because it was more convenient for a right handed helmsman.

The very best ship finds of actual Viking ships to date are the *Oseberg* and the *Gokstad* ships, named after the districts on Oslow Fjord where they were found. The Oseberg ship is about 70 feet long by about 17 feet beam, built with considerable strength but with the most delicate craftsmanship and decoration. She was apparently a type known as a Karvi, a small vessel used coastwise, for the private use of a local chief and his followers. As near as makes no difference, she was a yacht, and what could be more natural than that her owner should take her with him when he was buried. After all, it is only a few years since King George V had his favourite yacht, *Britannia,* scuttled after his death.

The Oseberg ship was built with 12 planks a side, could be rowed with fifteen pairs of oars and was fitted with a mast and sail. The Gokstad ship is a little longer, 76 feet, with the same beam, deeper in the hull with sixteen planks a side and had sixteen pairs of oars. She is stronger, more seaworthy, and altogether a more sober ship than the Oseberg vessel, although she too was most likely the private karvi of a chief. She was built fifty years or so later than the Oseberg ship and it is tempting to read into her the additional experience of seafaring which would have come from the extensive Viking raiding excursions during that time. On the other hand, one can see as big a range of differences in neighbouring private yachts today and so it may only reflect the tastes of different owners.

It is perhaps the craftsmanship of these ships which takes the breath away. First is their design. It would be difficult these days with all the technology and computers available to design a better, large, open water rowing boat in terms of shape and, indeed, of structure. Second, however, is the sheer labour and skill of the manner in which they were put together. The Nydam ship, for instance, shows a typical planking arrangement where each plank is actually carved from a thicker one to leave projecting wooden lugs on the inside face. These were drilled to receive lashings by which each plank is bound to each rib. Again, look at the keels of the later ships which were carved for their full length to form a T or Y shape for the attachment of the first garboard planks. The Oseberg ship incorpor-

ates a carved L-shaped plank at the bottom of the topsides. All these had to be wrought by hand with primitive tools. Clincher planking itself is acknowledged as a craft skill pinnacle and, never have better examples been produced, than by the Vikings for their longboats.

Neither the Gokstad nor Oseberg ship appears to have been fitted with thwarts for the rowers and it has been suggested that they did in fact sit on their sea chests. The Gokstad ship was found with shields placed all round the shipside. As more elaborate securings than those found would be necessary, to keep the shields in place in bad weather, it seems that this accepted hallmark of the Viking raider might well have been a harbour parade item only.

During the Viking era their ships were measured by the number of *rums* or rooms they contained. These referred to the actual or nominal space between the thwarts. Each room in fact accounted for a pair of rowers, one port and one starboard. The normal ship, as required for occasional fuedal government use, would have had twenty rooms but ships with 25 or even 30 rooms were not unknown. The largest and finest Viking ship ever built, was said to be Olaf Tryggvason's *Long Serpent,* which was built in AD 99. Her keel length has been recorded as 114 feet, which meant that she must have been about 140 feet in length overall, and she is said to have had 34 oarsmen a side. King Canute, it is rumoured, had himself a 60 roomer but, if the normal conventions of size and proportions for the period are observed, she would have had to be about 250 feet in length. This would have been a prodigious feat, a *Great Eastern* of her day, for modern man was not ever able to push wooden vessels up to a much greater length. It is only the apparent skill and knowledge of the Norse boatbuilders which leaves one with a sneaking feeling that they might indeed have done it.

The longest ship actually recovered is the *Sutton Hoo* vessel, dating from somewhere about 650 AD. Since her ends were lost it is impossible to be exact, but it is thought that she was getting on for 90 feet in length with a beam of about 14 feet. She was

Right *This seal is from Winchelsea. It shows a ship without oars but with platforms at the end developed into little castellated forts. The town seals provide the only real illustrations of the sailing ship in the dark ages.*

Below *These details of the Bayeaux tapestry show the kind of ships used in the Norman invasion of England in 1066.*

clincher built, in the classic manner, with nine strakes a side and carried twenty pairs of oarsmen. One of the most impressive features of the remains, apart from the treasures which were buried with her, are the beautifully made iron rivets which were used to fasten the planking.

From the enormous factual detail of the Viking relics, we run into something like a brick wall right up into the middle of the fifteenth century. At the beginning of the period we have, fortunately, the Bayeux tapestry which, while showing the life history of Harold II, fortuitously includes graphic pictures of his shipwreck and of the Norman invasion fleet.

Essentially the Bayeux ships, both Norman and Saxon, look very much like the Viking craft. They appear to be shorter and fatter but as they still show sixteen oars a side they cannot be very far from the Gokstad ship in proportions. All the ships appear to be clincher built, to carry a single steering oar to starboard, and to set a single simple squaresail. Probably, the Viking ships were of such excellent form that they provided an unassailable pattern. However, small differences in detail can be seen. First is the curious manner in which the Saxon ships have a break in their top strake amidships, with the rowers also missing in this area. Both fleets are now using raised platforms in the ends of the vessel, probably initially built there to improve the fighting qualities, but probably prized by the master for his command bridge and his lookouts. The sails are now set with bowlines instead of the Scandinavian bearing-out spar but although highly decorated, the sails are shown as if they were extremely baggy. In fact they are shown looking like funnel shaped triangular bags with but a single sheet at the foot, but this is probably an exaggeration. Every ship is shown with a golden wind vane at the masthead, yet another indication of the importance of windward sailing, for the windvane is not terribly important sailing downwind with a squaresail. Duke William, as befits the leader, carries a lantern at his masthead in addition to his sailing vane.

After this, we are more or less dependent on the

Left The Hastings Common Seal. An early 14th century town seal which shows a ship with a single castle aft.

Left The seal of Sandwich dated about 1238 shows a mast head top or crow's nest and a dinghy on board.

Above *This detail from a painting by Holbein shows a Hanseatic ship. The picture is dated about 1532.*

town seals of the ports, for any illumination on the progress of the sailing ship in the dark ages. The *Winchelsea* seal, for instance, shows a ship without oars but with the platforms at the ends developed into little castellated forts. The *Hastings* seal shows a ship with a single castle aft but, more important, shows her with several sets of reef points and, a good set of shrouds angled aft. This infers very strongly, that ships of this time were essentially sailing ships. The size of the sail could be readily reefed or unreefed to suit wind conditions on a long voyage and the yard could be braced well round for windward sailing. The seal of *Sandwich,* dated to about 1238, shows a masthead top or crow's nest, which may indicate an interest in offshore navigation and also shows a dinghy on board.

They are all drawn with considerable sheer and clincher planking, following the Norse model, but there is a feeling that they are getting shorter. The only guidance we have is that whereas the classic proportions of the Viking ship gave about five beams to length, those for the Middle Ages stayed close to three beams to length for many years. It

seems more than likely that the transition would occur at the same time as the transition in emphasis from rowing propulsion to sail.

The next real advance in sailing must be the introduction of the stern hung rudder. The replacement of a steering oar, lashed to the side of the ship with a mechanism, a rudder hinged with iron working parts to the stern, was not only a revolution in thinking at sea, but also an opening of the door to the transom sterned boat. This type was always suspect before, because of the offsetting of the single rudder. The first example actually pictured is thought to be in a plaster painting in *Fide Church* in Gotland, from the thirteenth century. She is shown with the tiller carried forward in a loop around the high stern post, presumably to give the helmsman a steering sensation not dissimilar to that of the side rudder, with which he would be familiar. The actual efficiency of the centre hung rudder may well have come as a surprise however. The seal of *Poole,* dated 1325, also shows a ship with a stern hung rudder and, after that they began to be in common usage.

Right *A 16th century port, showing ships at anchor and some aspects of the busy port life. The rigging of the ships is the most interesting aspect.*

2

5

6

One of the most important sailing ships of the period was the *Hanseatic cog*, a trading vessel used by the great merchant league based on Northern Europe. A wreck thought to be a cog has been dug out of the river bed at *Bremen* and is still being investigated. Meanwhile for some idea of the cog we are again mostly restricted to town seals. That from the port of *Elbing* shows a deep straight ended vessel with a single mast although also fitted with either an elongated stempost or a bowsprit, to extend the bowlines during windward sailing. The stern platform or castle has now become an integral part of the hull and the forward castle is retained. The hull shape, heavy shrouds, and deep construction show that this is a merchant ship, perhaps a 100 feet long, probably carrying a very large sail.

There has been much speculation about the origins of the cog, but it seems possible that some kind of similar craft had been in use, as a general workhorse for years, avoiding the limelight and the illustrations of the warships and ships of chiefs. A comparatively small ship found at *Graveney* on the south banks of the Thames, dated to somewhere about 900 AD shows similar hull shape characteristics, at least as far as can be guessed from the portion recovered. Originally she must have been about 46 feet in length with a beam of less than 10 feet. She was massively built of oak, with the planking clenched with iron nails. Other evidence suggests that she was used as a general purpose cargo vessel. It is possible that she may originally have been fitted with masts and sails but these were abandoned, and it seems that she spent a great deal of her working life being rowed.

It would be natural, for the merchants of the Hanseatic league, to employ existing craft rather than to set out to develop a new type. It is equally natural, that the commercial pressures of a trading empire, probably started a building programme, with competition among builders and seamen for ships with good performance, resulting perhaps in the establishment of the cog as a particular type.

The wrecks of Bremen and Graveney show the development of cogs

It seems remarkable, that apart from the use of the artemon by the Romans, there was little in the way of a multiple sailing rig in general European use, right up to the fifteenth century. Presumably, in Northern Europe, the overwhelming excellence of the Viking/Scandinavian ship blanketed the picture, until ships suddenly began to get bigger. Up until the fifteenth century, ships were comparatively small, up to a hundred feet or so approximately, clincher built and double ended. The stern post was now straight, to carry the rudder hangings and, the stern castle was more or less built as part of the hull, possibly with a small transom over the rudder. The forecastle remained a small, triangular deck, perched up high and overhanging the bow. The single sail was much the same but the shrouds had got noticeably heavier.

The usual reasons for dividing a sail area into

Left These drawings of ships show the evolution of the sail plans of ships from 1430–1600.

1, A primitive late medieval cog. 2, 3, 4, Stages in the development of a merchant-man of the Carrack type. 5, 6, 16th century galleons.

smaller units are to ease the problems of handling each sail and of staying its mast. There are many other benefits however, extra efficiency, from the slot effects among sails and greater flexibility in controlling the ship when manoeuvring, but it seems most likely that the initial reasons, lay in the problems of powering much larger ships. Henry V is said for instance, to have built a 186 footer at Bayonne in 1419.

The two master, would seem to have been an obvious step from the single master. There are comparatively few illustrations of such craft from the period and ship building seems to have progressed in less than a hundred years, from one sail on one mast, to three sails or more, on three masts. The reason is probably one of balance. In a wide-bodied, more or less, double-ended ship, a mast in the middle of her length can be well supported with widely angled stays. Masts at the ends have a

narrower platform and therefore have to be shorter and carry smaller sails. A ship with a big squaresail and a small sail added forward would be basically unbalanced with the wind abeam and therefore a balancing sail would be required aft. It is interesting to note in this context that the English word mizzen for the after mast is derived from the same source as the French word *missaine* (the foremast) from the Arabic *mizan*, a balance or adjustment.

The earliest picture of a northern three master is probably a seal of about 1466, but by 1500 three masters were common. Not only that, but the sailing ship had grown in size and reliability. When first introduced the three master was fitted with a small square foresail, a large square mainsail, and a small lateen mizzen. By the time of Columbus, however, this had been further increased by a square topsail over the mainsail and another sail, like the artemon, under the bowsprit.

The parallel development of ships in the Mediterranean starts with a six hundred year blank period. The first glimpses come from two ninth century manuscripts where bible stories are illustrated with ship drawings presumably showing contemporary craft. These are drawn very much like Roman ships, with twin steering oars, but with lateen sails. The lateen is thought to be a sail of Arabic origin, probably stemming from the more rigorous sailing required offshore between the Arabian Gulf, Africa and India. Its characteristics are essentially a triangular sail setting on a very long yard, which is supported on a short mast, usually raking forward. It is set to windward, with the yard raking upwards from the stemhead, to form a long luff similar to the Bermudan sail and of high efficiency. Running, the yard is often braced up horizontally, with the greater sail area catching the higher wind. It suffers from the long length of the yard and from the need when tacking, to pass the sail right around in front of the yard which has to be rolled over the masthead, but all in all, in skilled hands it is one of the most efficient rigs ever produced.

The Ports of Genoa, Pisa and Venice, thronged with shipping

More details of the Mediterranean sailing ships, come from the chroniclers of the Crusades, when Genoa, Pisa and Venice were the principal embarkation ports. In general form the Romans would have recognised them. The twin steering oars still persisted and in fact, were not superseded by the rudder until the fourteenth century. The steering oars were contained inside galleries or wings which swept out aft and which ran on up through the aft castles, to make a pair of horns. These were the equivalent of what we would nowadays call a boom gallows and were used to contain and support the long and cumbersome lateen yard when it was lowered onto the deck. In rig they were becoming two-masters with the artemon sail getting larger and larger.

The central rudder and the squaresail both appeared in the Mediterranean together about the fourteenth century. Perhaps the squaresail had not wholly disappeared, but its reappearance in first class ships has all the hallmarks of a reintroduction from the northern vessels. Perhaps it was the contact with the crusaders, but one source declares that it was due to an invasion of pirates from the Atlantic.

The Mediterranean ships, which explored and traded outside the Pillars of Hercules, more or less went over the squaresail and developed in a similar style to the Northern ship. It is likely that the carrack became the southern equivalent of the cog but with carvel planking instead of clincher and still showing a touch of the Roman fatness about her after quarters compared with the general balance between forward and aft of the northern craft. The carracks shown in fifteenth century paintings carry a square mainsail and a lateen mizzen while the bowsprit appears, as yet, to be untenanted and used only for the bowlines of the mainsail. The

Left This picture from a 15th century Italian Bible depicts the apostles of Christ fishing at sea. The vessel is a good example of a small 15th century ship.

Below This early drawing of Italy's chief port, Genoa shows the busy traffic in the harbour at this time and the types of shipping that traded there. In this picture both rowing galleys and merchant ships can be seen.

Bottom Venice was also a thriving mercantile port at this time. This woodcut is dated about 1480 and once again shows the variety of the 15th century merchant ships.

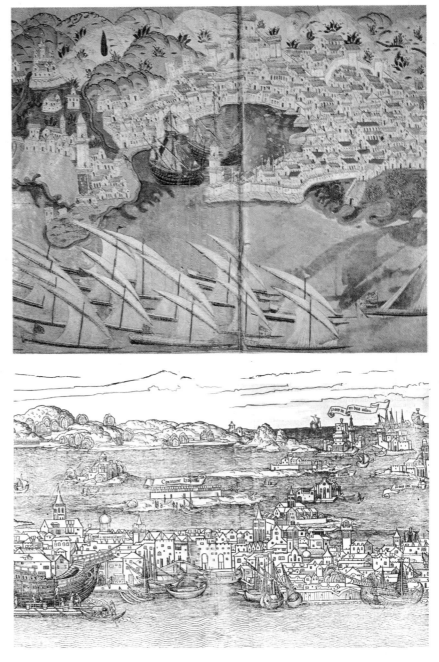

Right A 15th century carrack from an engraving by a Dutch master.

Below A number of medieval craft showing the great variety of rigs in common use.

lateen incidentally, is a very logical sail to carry on the mizzen for its prime purpose would be that of giving balance when the ship was reaching or on the wind. Downwind there would be little use for an aft sail, and quite the contrary in strong winds.

The only model ship known from the time is the *Mataro* ship now in Rotterdam Museum. Officially she is called a *Nao*, but this term probably has much the same meaning as the word ship in English and refers to a broad type. Experts think that she really represents a two-masted carrack. The model shows very clearly the amount of top hamper which was being built onto the original simple hull form. The aft castle now extends as a solid structure all the way to the mainmast amidships and the space below the forecastle has been boarded in as well. Further, on top of the stern castle is another platform and one can see in embryo the towering edifices which became such a feature of the Spanish galleon.

By the end of the fifteenth century the carrack had grown into a very enclosed vessel, often with a double forecastle deck and in fact only a small waist forward of amidships, still representing the original clear decks. Most interesting, however, in terms of rig development is that the shrouds are

The Mataro ship, a forerunner of the towering Spanish galleons

now taken outside the hull to projecting platforms called chains or channels from which they are braced with iron bars back to bolts through the shipside. The significance is either that the shipbuilders were attempting to increase sail area by means of taller masts or that they were attempting to decrease the hull beam for the same sail area. Both of these would be a result of a desire to increase the ship's sailing performance.

It is likely that Columbus' *Santa Maria* was a carrack but he was not very complimentary about her and only calls her a nao. He mentions that she set a spritsail – a small sail set under the bowsprit – and that she did occasionally make use of the dinghy sail, set on the dinghy while it was still on its chocks on board. All told, however, it is clear that Columbus preferred the caravel type of his other two ships.

The origin of the caravel is not clear and in fact there are few details of it. Henry the Navigator mostly used caravels for his voyages of discovery and they appear to have been light, strong, seaworthy craft with long rounded bows, hollow waterlines and with transom sterns. Generally they were rigged with two or three lateen sails with the largest one forward. They carried no forward castle but a comparatively long aftercastle built into the hull and it is thought they might have been about 70 feet in length with a beam of about 20 feet. The only possible relic of the caravel to be seen may be the fregatas, which are still to be found on the Tagus working as river barges, for there remains about them something of a resemblance to the old sketches and drawings of caravels.

Below *The Portuguese conquered with a cross in one hand and a sword in the other. They were famous for their conquests in the Indian ocean. This early 16th century painting, by Cornelius Anthonissn, depicts Portuguese ships of war.*

Chapter IV
The voyagers

Herodotus, born about 490 BC, reports that a hundred years or so earlier Africa was circumnavigated by the Phoenicians. The expedition was sent out by the Pharaoh Necho on the 15,000 mile voyage and returned via the Straits of Gibraltar, two or three years later. It was a long journey for sailors who probably tried at least to spend each night ashore and who even followed the natural rhythm of the seasons by staying ashore to grow crops along the way. As happens to travellers so often, on their return much of their account of their adventures was disbelieved. Herodotus himself, although he reports it, feels that it cannot be true that when they were at the southern tip of Afr the sun was to the north of them. This knowledge would only be available to a traveller who had penetrated well south of the equator and points out the unique nature of this early expedition, particularly as the Phoenicians did not have the compass. Very few other remarkable passages are recorded between this expedition and those of Bartolomeo Dias some two thousand years later.

We know, also from Herodotus, of the sad story of Sataspes of Samos who, in punishment for a crime, was sent by Xerxes to sail round Africa in an anticlockwise direction. The bulge of Africa proved too much for him and after meeting dwarfs clad in palm leaves at his furthest point south, he returned

Each maritime power, treasured its seafaring secrets

to face the alternative punishment which was impalement. We know from his account of Hanno of Carthage's remarkable colonizing voyage of about 500 BC. He was commissioned to found colonies and set out with sixty ships, each with fifty oars, filled with colonists, stores and equipment. He sailed through the Straits of Gibraltar and along the Moroccan coast, dropping off groups of colonists. From his account, it is possible to trace a journey which took him past Cape Verde to the Guinea coast. He describes his ships as pentecosters, fast 50 oared galleys which were principally used for sea raiding in packs. Their use rather than the use of the commodious merchantmen which would seem more natural for carrying all the goods required to establish colonies indicated perhaps that they were more frightened of the unknown dangers of the sea voyage than they were of the hardships ashore. His voyage was in fact of a summer's duration only and he returned when his supplies ran out.

Although there is little precise documentary evidence of great exploratory voyages for the next two thousand years, it does not mean of course that they did not occur. Historical knowledge, depending as it does on the accidents of documentary survival and other evidence, must inevitably be patchy. We can be fairly certain that voyaging did not stop for that would be unnatural, but it is certain that countries tended to regard information about trade routes and foreign ports, as important secrets of great commercial value. It is likely therefore that each new maritime power, Egyptian, Grecian, Roman, Arabian or Christian, treasured its own information and tended to disregard that of the previous regime. In the same way individual mariners were jealous of their geographical knowledge which represented the secrets of their own craft at a time when craftsmen in general hugged their trades tightly to them. It is unlikely, therefore, that seamen would lightly offer their knowledge to scholars, who might have recorded it for posterity. Thus, information was not recorded until spurred by the occasional far-seeing and powerful personality such as Ptolemy, Prince Henry the Navigator and Hakluyt, that any real pooling of knowledge of sea routes took place.

It is often quoted that Columbus' crew were frightened of falling over the edge of the world, which they believed to be a flat dish. It seems unlikely that seamen who must have been accustomed to the sight of ships and indeed land appearing and disappearing over the horizon would be serious about such a possibility; especially since Ptolemy of Alexander, who collated his famous treatise on geography about 150 AD, had shown the world to be round. There was a similar belief stretching as far back as to the days of the Babylonians. It is more likely that Columbus's men were making an early version of the standard seaman's joke about falling off the edge of the chart or getting caught in its fold.

The next outburst of exploratory voyaging of which we know occurred in the fifteenth century, principally based on the Portuguese exploration inspired by Prince Henry. At that time there was a reasonable basis of information about much of the world. Europe, the near east and the northern part of Africa were tolerably mapped and there was information on India and China, and even a tiny suspicion about the possibility of an America. There was still 'Terra Incognita' in plenty however, to be explored for booty, trade and even evangelizing.

Prince Henry set up at Sagres in the south west of Portugal a centre for the investigation and correlation of all seafaring knowledge: the ships, the seas they sailed upon, instruments and charts. More important, he made the knowledge collected accessible to all seafarers. He gathered round him the best navigators, cartographers, astrologers, shipbuilders, and seamen, and he despatched expeditions to fill in specific gaps in the information available. His explorers voyaged in the main along the west coast of Africa and to the Azores, Canaries and Cape Verde Islands. In addition to knowledge of local

1427, the discovery of the Azores, a turning point in navigation

conditions in each area they were also seeking a new sea route to India, avoiding the Arab dominated route down the Red Sea and across the Indian Ocean.

The discovery of the Azores by the Portuguese in 1427 marked a turning point in ocean navigation, for they are in a zone where variable winds meet the trade winds. The Portuguese in their caravels became confident in making long tacks out to sea, as they penetrated further and further south. On returning they would keep the trade winds on the beam until they reached the latitude of the Azores when they turned east and homewards in the prevailing westerlies.

Prince Henry sent out two or three expeditions every year but there was considerable reluctance to pass south of Cape Bojador, now called Cape Juby, for they believed, and who could blame them, that there the sea was boiling and the sun would turn a man black. Prince Henry specifically sent a nobleman, Gil Eanes, to round the Cape and so disprove this in 1434, and when another expedition a few

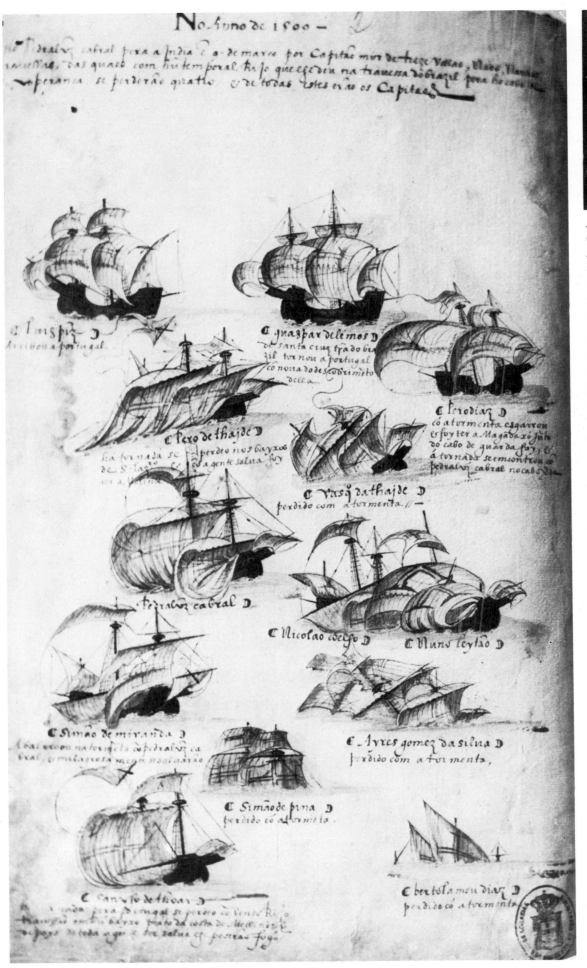

No Anno de 1500 —

Above *A portrait by Gaudos of Henry the Navigator. All the fame that Portugal gained on the high seas in the 15th and 16th centuries can be traced to his intelligence and foresight. The discoveries made by his captains led directly to Da Gama's rounding of the Cape and his discovery of sea routes to India.*

Left *This page from the Livros das Armadas shows the various ships comprising the Armada of Pedro Alvarez Cabral which by missing India altogether, sailed across the Pacific and discovered Brazil by accident. The Livros is a 16th century record of what happened to each fleet on its way to the East.*

Top *This Ptolemic map was used for navigation in the period of the great explorations of the 15th and 16th centuries.*

Above *An impression of a 16th century bireme.*

Right *A detail of the Cantino map of 1502 showing the Portuguese fort of San Jorge de Mina, on the Guinea coast, which was once visited by Columbus.*

Os montes claros em affrica:

terra dell Rey organe o qual
Rey he muy nobre muito Rico

terra del Rey de nubia o qual
Rey sempre trace contynada
mente guerra conzl pretoh̄a
o qual Rey he monzo remuyto
ap̃smigno de caftrios

Serra lioa:

Castello damina

e̅ra esta serra lioa amuyto ouxe este
he omuis fino que ay em mahua
parte 2traentem pa portigall 2 mintos
escraba deles sam dgchof 2dolẽ 19 de
mandiga 1 doi cope 2 estei
tas miu
hoas 2
panos
dalgo
da

dondetracemaomuyto
o̅ sotente princpe dom mamuell R̃,y̅ de portugall cada anno voze caza
belas cam piua̅ tuazeedacarabre byla co ontra xẽb mjll pesos
douro bal cada yeſſo su jnhantos lf uas 1mois tracm umiptos
eſſzbos 2 pinteyta ro h̄ı˜tra e teas˜ſ 6s de muyto
ṗoneita

terra del Principe

ṕta delga de
do garo
Rio do boſto
serra guerreira
pi˜ do aco garias
Rio do goppo
plaia do mede˜e
Rio de Conbeliso
de San Juan
rio do arbiſo

Far right A portrait by an unknown contemporary artist, of the famous explorer Vasco da Gama. His discoveries added to the astonishing achievement of the Portuguese in the 15th and 16th centuries.

No Annode. 524.

Partio dom Vasq̃ dagama conde Almirante primeyro descobridor da Jndia por Viso Rey della. et anoue dabril (com hūa Armada de quatorze naos) se fez aa Vella. et sendo com a frota das ditas vellas, junto da costa da Jndia et tremeo Ro mar Rũ quarto dóra, et com temor esbonbardearão hūas ás outras das quaes esteberão os capitaes

Ropovaz de sã payo
pera coesim

Do simão de meneses

Dom fernão de morro
perdose em Melinde et saluouse agente; Ria po ca pitão de goa.

Dom Vasq̃ da gama

Fco de saõ

Antº da silueyra

Pº mas carenhas
pera malaca

christouão Rosado
perdido

Dom Anxrique de meneses

Francisqº de brito
perdido

Ruy glz̃

Lopo lobo

Mossem gaspar
por ser sp̃o estrangr̃ armadar mayo donecessario agente da caranella selenancu cotracke et so matarã

Afonsso mexia
por veador da fz̃da

Right The famous Livros das Armadas gives us a fine record of the many Portuguese vessels of this period. This page shows the Armada of Vasco da Gama.

66

they proved to be the real basis for most of the fifteenth century exploration.

After Prince Henry the Navigator's death in 1460 his nephew King John II of Portugal continued with the search for a route round the south of Africa to the wealth of the Indies. In 1487 he sent out Bartolomeo Dias in a modest fleet of two caravels, each of about 100 tons, plus an additional storeship. Dioas managed to get well south towards the Cape, when he was caught in a strong northerly gale. By the time he had struggled back to land he

The development of shipping owes much to the Kings of Portugal

had passed the southern tip of Africa, which he feelingly named Cape Tempestuous. On his return to Lisbon, King John took a different view of the occasion and renamed it the Cape of Good Hope. In 1495, King Manual of Portugal too was obsessed with the trade routes to India and ordered Vasco da Gama to prepare another expedition. Dias himself designed two of the ships, the *Sao Gabriel* and the *Sao Raphael,* each of about 120 tons, altering the standard caravel model for the bad weather to be expected off the Cape. Illustrations of the period show them as being rigged with three masts, a single squaresail on the foremast, squaresail and square-topsail on the main, and a lateen mizzen. In fact the conventional ship rig of the day. Perhaps the modification was to apply the more easily handled ship rig, to the more easily driven caravel hull and this may have been one of the early steps in the development of the galleon. The other two ships were the small caravel *Berrio* and a large storeship.

Vasco da Gama set off in July 1497 and made first for the Cape Verde Islands. Then instead of the soul-destroying crawl down the African coast, among the baffling and changeable winds he set boldly off to sail well out into the Atlantic, on a route which was later proved ideal by the clipper ships. He took a broad sweep, arriving back at the African coast in November right into Table Bay. Then he punched the headwinds around the Cape and up the west coast all the way to Mombasa, before striking across the Indian Ocean to Calicut. The return journey was an ordeal of scurvy, and by the time he re-passed the Cape he had only two ships left and when he eventually returned to Lisbon after two years he had only 55 men left from the 170 who sailed with him. Vasco da Gama was piloted across the Indian Ocean by an Arab navigator and the Arabs had a well established trade with India. The Chinese also traded with India and East Africa, so in addition to establishing the Portuguese trade route to India, the expedition formed one of the first direct sea links between Europe and the Far East itself.

Christopher Columbus was one of the many fifteenth century seamen who dreamed of reaching the wealth of the Indies. After that route was proved and established, it became clear that there would be no further sponsorship from Portugal. Perhaps with Ptolemy's map, which had been re-published in

years later brought back gold and slaves, enthusiasm redoubled.

Gil Eanes sailed in a *barcos*, presumably a ship, and another voyager, Baldaia, in a *varinel*, and both are described as 'heavy vessels and difficult to manoeuvre, broad in the beam and lying low in the water.' The rig is not mentioned, but it is clear that these ships were not popular for this kind of work. Prince Henry promoted the use of the caravel for his explorations. It appears to have been used previously for transport around the coast of Portugal and as an offshore fishing boat. When he set up his school at Sagres, Henry deliberately chose a place as near as possible to Cape St. Vincent where 'the Mediterranean and the Great Ocean combat one another' and had unrivalled opportunities for

Caravels, beautiful and intriguing, the basis of 15th century exploration

selecting the best possible vessels to send out on his voyages. It was likely therefore, that they would start with the vessels they saw every day, coping well with the rough Atlantic seas.

The caravels they used were in fact, improved versions, increased in length, tonnage and in sails. They were rigged with two and later three lateen sails, set with the largest forward and in decreasing order of size aft, to give one of the most efficient windward working rigs ever devised. Not only was each sail of beautiful aerodynamic form, but the grouping gave a double slot effect which increases the the efficiency quite remarkably, an effect reinvented by Handley Page and other aircraft pioneers, nearly five hundred years later. These beautiful and intriguing ships can only be found by reference in old manuscripts and the occasional thumbnail drawing on a chart or rather indistinct picture, but

Right This illustration shows a map of the world after 1492. It is interesting in that it shows the South Pole at the top.

Far right A contemporary picture of Columbus taking observations of the sun.

Centre A portrait of Christopher Columbus by an unknown artist. Columbus made many voyages of exploration though he is most famous for his discovery of America.

Right One of Columbus' ships drawn from a contemporary woodcut.

1477, he turned his attention to Spain and to the possibilities of a westard route to the Indies. In 1492 he set off on his voyage with three ships, the ship rigged *Santa Maria* and the caravels *Nina* and *Pinta,* and more or less found America across his path. Whether his discovery of the continent is predated by Lief Ericsson in Viking times, or by his contemporary Amerigo Vespucci is not really important. Columbus set off without prior knowledge of this enormous barrier between him and his goal.

Christopher Columbus, unhappy with his ships, discovered America

Experts seem to be agreed, that the Santa Maria was a small carrack, probably only about 80 feet in length, with a beam of about 26 feet, carrying a total sail area of about 3,500 square feet. Small as this ship appears to have been, Columbus felt that she had been forced on him against his will. He apparently thought that she was too slow and difficult to manoeuvre and of too deep a draught to explore unknown coastlines. At any rate she was soon lost after her arrival and her leaky but immortal timbers used for building a fort. His other two ships were small caravels. The Pinta, is said to have been about 50 tons and the Nina rather less. The Pinta, incidentally, had her lateen sails replaced with squaresails in the Canary Islands and, there is no doubt that for a downwind trade wind passage from the Canaries to the West Indies, the squaresail is a much better rig than a lateen. The Pinta and the Nina arrived safely back home independently. For his next expedition, when he could choose his fleet, Columbus set off with no less than fourteen caravels and only three carracks. To his death, he thought that he had found a new corner of the Indies rather than a new continent. The Pope in recognition of the eastward influence of the Portuguese and the westward influence brought to the Spanish by Columbus, promptly divided the world between them, either as outright titles to new lands, or at least as uncontested semi-spheres of influence.

In 1519 Magellan was sent to make good the Spanish claim to the West. Charles V gave him a fleet of five ships of which we know little except their names and tonnages – *Santo Antonio*, 120 tons, *Trinidad*, 110 tons, *Concepcion*, 90 tons, *Victoria*, 85 tons, and *Santiago*, 75 tons. It is likely that they were three masted galleons. Magellan had undertaken to find a way past the barrier of America so that the Spanish could get at the Spice Islands of the Moluccas which they coveted. His voyage was beset with problems, a mutiny, a ship wreck, and a ship desertion, all before he had navigated the extremely difficult Straits named after him and found his way into the Pacific. Then, unprepared for the vastness of the Pacific, they suffered enormous privations during the four month voyage, which brought them to the Phillipines, where Magellan himself was killed in a fracas with the natives. It is ironic that the first man to round the world was in fact Magellan's Moluccan slave, who achieved this record when the fleet reached his

native islands. It is equally ironic that the sole ship of the five which left Spain to return to Seville, was the *Victoria* under the command of one of the mutineers, Sebastian del Cano.

Magellan became famous as the first man to sail across the Pacific but undoubtedly the ocean was already well known and used by the Chinese, and even the colonizers among the Polynesian islanders. It is a natural tendency for us to view exploration entirely from our own point of view.

The English were not involved with this partition of new lands, since the discoveries coincided with Henry VIII's divorce from Catherine of Aragon and his consequent dispute with the Pope. Francis Drake, determined to acquire both booty and demonstrate the practical precariousness of the Spanish claim to the Pacific, set sail in 1577. Like Magellan, Drake started out with five ships, although in general they were much smaller. The flagship was the *Pelican,* later renamed the *Golden Hind.* No accurate dimensions are known for her but because of her fame, the ship was preserved for a hundred years in a dry dock at Deptford on her return and her size can be guessed from that of the dock. This gives her a length overall of about 75 feet to the tip of her beakhead and about 60 feet stem to sternpost. Her beam must have been about 19 feet and her depth in the hold around nine to ten feet, but all these dimensions are extremely arguable. The other ships in the little fleet were the *Elizabeth,* 80 tons, *Marigold,* 30 tons, *Swan,* 50 tons, and a pinnace, the *Benedict,* of 15 tons, which was later changed for a 40 ton ship they captured off the coast of Africa.

Like Magellan, Drake had to deal with mutiny, disaffection and the general frittering away of his fleet. A storm drove him south in sight of Cape Horn and proved that there was yet another route into the Pacific. His attacks on the Spaniards in the Pacific, however, were extremely successful and he was also able to keep his crew much healthier than Magellan. He sailed as far north as Vancouver, stopped for a while in California and then decided to sail back via the East Indies and the Cape of Good Hope. Finally he returned to England, with fame and with a fortune, at the end of 1580.

Whereas the fifteenth century had its Dias, da Gama and Columbus, and the sixteenth its Magellan and Drake to mark out and girdle the world, the seventeenth century produced fewer and less illustrious names. It was more a time for filling in the details of the map, and above all for opening up new trading regions. The first half really belongs to the Dutch East India company, which was founded in 1602 and rapidly became the most powerful force

The Dutch East India company gave its name to merchantmen

in the Malay archipeligo. This company was to keep a very tight hold on the area, holding secret their charting, surveying and exploring. Their ships represented their general martial methods of colonization and were very similar to the ships built for the Dutch navy. Three masted galleons with at least one row of guns, probably rigged with three squaresails each on the forward mast and main and a square topsail over a lateen on the mizzen, were typical of the ships they used. A spritsail would be set at the end of the bowsprit with possibly a sprit topsail set over it in the slightly unlikely style of the period.

One of the governors of the company, Anthony van Diemen, sent Abel Tasman on a voyage of exploration in 1642. His avowed object was simply that of 'finding the remaining unknown parts of the terrestrial globe.' With two ships, the *Heemskerck* and the *Zeehaen,* they circumnavigated Australia and thereby proved that it was an independent continent. They also looked at New Zealand but did not discover that it was in fact in two parts, nor did they discover the legendary southern continent for which they had been keeping one eye open. After that it was left to the buccaneers and privateers to explore and open up the sea lanes around the Pacific and William Dampier in particular left interesting journals of his navigations.

Left top The straits of Magellan were originally shown by map makers to be an open passage, when in fact they were narrow and twisting, as later exploration showed.

Left below A 16th century artist's impression of how the longitude of the earth can be found by deviation of a magnet from the Pole.

Centre This ship of only 85 tons was the first to sail around the world. One of Ferdinand Magellan's fleet of five it set sail in September 1519 and returned to Spain three years later.

Below A fleet of canoes which rowed out to meet Magellan's fleet in the Philippines.

Right *Sir Francis Drake, the famous English explorer set sail in 1577. He started out with five ships and sailed as far north as Vancouver, stopped for a while in California and then decided to sail back via the East Indies and the Cape of Good Hope. He returned to England in 1580.*

Science and trade had become by the eighteenth century, the twin inspirations of the civilized world and this prompted further official and more detailed exploration with the British Admiralty, for one, providing men, money and ships. The search for the semi-mythical southern continent continued and when Cook was ordered to the Pacific to take scientists to Tahiti, to observe the transit of Venus. His further orders were to go south to look for the elusive south land. Comparatively few explorers are actually allowed to choose their craft, most having to take what their sponsors will spare. Cook however was given a free hand and it is hardly surprising that he should select a Whitby collier, since he was a Yorkshireman who first went to sea in that class of ship. His choice fell on a simple little collier called the *Earl of Pembroke*. She was slightly rebuilt

Cooke, in his ship the Endeavour Bark charted the South Pacific

for the voyage and was renamed *Endeavour Bark* to avoid confusion with an *Endeavour* already on the navy list. Her plans are preserved from the Admiralty draughts for the alterations. She was built in 1764 and she was therefore only four years old when she was bought for Cook and was in every way a typical bluff, bowed, extremely simple, three masted vessel without the grace of a figurehead or beakhead or other decoration. She was somewhere about 100 feet in length with 30 feet beam and with 11 feet depth of hold. She is described as a cat-built bark, implying that she had full waterlines at the stern tapering off into a comparatively narrow transom at deck level.

Cook did not in fact find any new continents, but the detailed surveying and chart work that he did, of lands and places only touched upon by previous explorers, is classic and still in use. He circumnavigated New Zealand and charted the east coast of Australia. He was nearly wrecked off Queensland on a coral reef and discovered the Great Barrier Reef before sailing for home in 1771.

Still the great southern continent was not discovered and the Admiralty sent him off again the following year. This time he had two ships, the *Resolution* and the *Adventure*. Again he chose Whitby colliers which were purchased by the Admiralty and altered slightly for his use. The *Resolution* emerged with a figurehead and a proper stern cabin for the commander, looking more like a warship, but the *Adventure* remained a true collier bark. This second voyage was perhaps the most remarkable. In 1773 they crossed the Antarctic circle, the first ships ever known to have done so. The ships were later separated and Cook made several forays into southern waters, rediscovering South Georgia and discovering several other islands. In 1775 Cook returned home after sailing 60,000 miles and, a most notable achievement for the time, having lost not a single crew member from scurvy. Throughout this voyage, he also used a chronometer to make precisely timed observations, thereby establishing that it was possible on a long

voyage to achieve accurate enough timing for calculations of longitude. Accurate timing such as this had been a dream of seamen ever since astronomical observations started to be used for sea navigation.

Cook's final voyage, again in the *Resolution*, but this time accompanied by the *Discovery*, took him first to the south and then north to the Bering sea and Alaska in search of the northwest passage. He returned to the Hawaiian Islands where he was killed by natives. *Resolution* and *Discovery* returned to England in 1780.

In the nineteenth century exploration was less on a global scale and grew even more scientific. It concentrated on the extension and the cataloguing of existing knowledge and surveying and charting of the remoter areas, the Poles, and the northwest passage, and a growing interest in marine biology.

There was also a commercial urge to open up new markets in a time of comparative peace and affluence and to give occupation for the naval officers, men and ships, previously engaged in the European wars. Later the need to survey routes for the new signalling telegraph cables across the sea beds added another dimension to the explorations.

In 1818 four small whaling ships set off on explorations to the north. They were not particularly successful but they carried between them men who were to become renowned polar explorers. The *Trent* and the *Dorothea* were bound for Spitzbergen and towards the North Pole, commanded by John Franklin. The *Isabella* and the *Alexander* were bound to look for the northwest passage around the top of the American continent. The *Isabella* was commanded by John Ross with his nephew James Clark Ross as a midshipman on

Far right *Drake's flagship the Golden Hind, was originally called the Pelican. She was about 75 feet to the tip of her beakhead, and about 60 feet stem to sternpost. Her beam must have been about 19 feet and her depth in the hold about 9 to 10 feet. She is shown here taking the Cara Fuego.*

Caca Fogo.

Caca Plato.

Below Ships trading in the East Indies, from a painting by H C Vroom, 1566-1640, a very early expedition of the East Indiamen.

H	K	IK	Courses	Winds	Tuesday Jan.y 12th 1768					H	K	HK
2	3	1	W.N.W.	S.r	The first part thick foggy W.r with little wind growing					2	4	...
4	3	1	N.W.b.W.	N.W.b.W.	out 1.t & 2.d Reef Topsails					4	2	1
6	3	1			Spoke a Snow call'd the Portland George Higgins Mr from Chas Town					6	1	1
8	3	1	W.b.N.½N.	S.W.	bound to Cowes... at 10 P.M. Strong Gales down M.r T'yards					8		Calm
10	4				at 12 in all R.M.'s handed Mizen T.s at 2 M.E.M.'s S.E.S.t					10		
12	3	1			at 8 M Reef'd the F.S.l Set it					12	1	1
2	4	1	W.b.N.	S.r b.S.t		Thick Wr		Co.r	S.W.½W.	2	2	1
4	4					No Observ.		Dis.t	76	4	4	
6	2							D.Latt.	23 N.o	6	4	
8	2					Tate. M.		Dep.t	70 W.	8	4	1
10	2		W.N.W.	S.W.		Account		D.Long.s	1. 47.10	10	5	
12	2					18. 41 N.o		Long. in 13.13		12	10	
	76	plo.s						Mer. Dis. 330 W.			71	Miles
								Long. M.s 8.33				

H	K	IK	Courses	Winds	Wednesday January 13th 1768					H	K	IK
2	2	...	W.b.N.	S.r b.S.t	The first and latter parts of this 24 hours Strong					2	5	...
4	2	...			Gales with heavy Squalls. the Middle it has Blown a					4	5	1
6	2	1	W.N.W.	S.W.	hard Storm with a very lofty dangerous Sea Running					6	4	
8	2	...			at 8 P.M. handed Main Sail Lay too under y.e Reef'd F.S.					8	4	1
10			up W.b.N.	off N.W.	at 8 A.M. Set Mr Sail Something moderate. a sail in sight by S.					10	3	
12			up N.W.b.W.	off N.W.b.W.						12	2	
2			up N.W.	off N.W.		Latt. Obs.d Ag.t N.o 3		Co.r	N.W.b.N.	2	2	1
4			up N.W.b.W.	off N.W.b.W.				Dis.t	36	4	3	1
6			up d.o	d.o				D.Latt.	22 N.o	6	5	
8	2	1	N.W.b.N.	W.b.S.t				Depart.	28 W.	8	4	
10	2	1	N.W.b.W.	N.W.b.W.				D.Long.	43 d.o	10	4	
12	2		N.N.W.	West.t				Long. in	13. 56	12	4	
	31	Mo.s						Mer. Dis.	358		96	Miles
								Long. M.s	9. 16			

H	K	IK	Courses	Winds	Thursday January 14th 1768					H	K	IK
2	1	1	N.W.	N.W.	Wore Ship. Strong Gales. at 4 P.M. out Reef F.S.					2	3	
			South	N.N.W.	the Middle Squally with heavy Showers of Rain & hail							
4	3	1	S.½E.		at 4 A.M. set S. at 6 d.o Set Mizen Topsail Mr T'yards & Jib					4	2	
6	2	1	South		the latter part Moderate Gales at 10 A.M. out 3 R.T.s					6	2	1
8	2	1	S.b.W.	W.b.S						8	2	
10	2	1								10	2	
12	2	1	South	W.S.W.				Co.r	N.46.W.	12	3	
2	2	1						Dist.	70.	2	3	
4	2	1	S.b.W.	W.b.S.				D.Latt.	54 N.o	4	2	1
6	3		S.S.W.	West.t				Depar.	44 East.	6	2	1
8	3							D.Long.	1. 7 d.o	8	1	
10	3	1						Long. in	12. 49 W.	10	5	
12	3	1						Mer. Dis.	314 d.o	12	6	
								L.M.	8. 9			

board. The *Alexander* was commanded by William Parry. The *Isabella,* incidentally, later saved the Rosses and their men after they had spent four winters in the Arctic and lost their own ship, the *Victory* an 85 ton steam packet, in the ice, following their discovery of the north magnetic pole.

The following year, 1819, Parry set off with two new ships, the *Hecla* and the *Griper,* with James Clark Ross serving with him, again for the north-west passage. Although they failed to find it, they penetrated further west than anyone before. Further expeditions in 1821 and 1824 did no better. In 1827 Parry set off, again with James Clark Ross in the crew, in *Hecla* towards the North Pole. *Hecla* was left at Spitzbergen and Parry and Ross set out in two specially converted ship's boats, *Enterprise* and *Endeavour,* flat bottomed to resist ice pressure and fitted with metal runners to go over the ice. Unfortunately man-handling these two ton craft over broken ice proved much more difficult than they expected and to crown it all, they found that the ice itself was drifting in a strong southerly current and had to abandon their gallant attempt. Expeditions of this nature, which might be labelled failures in their avowed intention, nevertheless brought back information on hundreds of miles of new territory, very often fully charted and described.

With the arrival of iron ships, an urgent need had arisen to investigate the earth's magnetism, to ensure the accuracy of the more delicate compasses which were required. Among other expeditions the British Admiralty despatched Captain James Clark Ross with *HMS Terror* of 340 tons and *HMS*

Erebus of 370 tons to find and plot the south magnetic pole. Both ships had been bomb ketches and were very heavily built to withstand the shock of firing big guns. They were further strengthened for the ice and Ross, from his previous experience of arctic work, is said to have had the provisions stowed so as to form a solid mass inside the holds. Bomb ketches were never designed for handy sailing, although their great beam allowed them to carry all plain sail in half a gale of wind. Their bluff bows and coarse lines made them both slow and difficult to steer. In their four year expedition, they took numerous observations while they explored the Antarctic in general. They discovered and named Victoria Land, the Ross Sea, Mount Erebus, Mount Terror, and the Ross Ice Barrier.

Erebus and *Terror* were later fitted with steam engines and took Sir John Franklin on his last and ill-fated expedition to look for the northwest passage in 1845. None of the 129 men survived and the two vessels disappeared completely, except for a mysterious sighting on an early morning in April 1851, when the English brig *Renovation* met an iceflow off the Newfoundland Banks, carrying with it two three-masted ships whose description fitted *Erebus* and *Terror.*

In 1831 a 90 foot three master, *HMS Beagle,* classed as a 10 gun brig of 242 tons, left Plymouth on what was a more or less routine voyage. Its mission was to chart some more of the South American coast and to carry out a chain of chronological reckonings right around the world. It is significant of the general interest in science at this time, that it was not thought very remarkable to

Above Botany Bay at the time of Cook's exploration. He chose Whitby colliers as his ships, which were bought by the Admiralty, and altered for his use.

Left A page from the Chronicle of the voyage from Bristol to Carolina.

include a naturalist and an artist in the crew of 74, to report and note anything of interest they might come across on the voyage. The Beagle voyage is notable because the naturalist was Charles Darwin who, despite sea-sickness, kept a passionate and close interest in everything he saw over the whole five years she was away. It is also indicative of the standards of accurate timing required by the voyage that the Beagle carried not less than 22 chronometers all packed away with great care in beds of sawdust.

The new dimension in exploration was the depth of the ocean and the voyage of the *Challenger* in

1872/76 brought its importance to public attention. It was inspired principally by the work of *HMS Lightning* and *HMS Porcupine* when surveying routes for the new submarine cables. The depths and conditions recorded in these surveys astonished the scientists of the day, and the Royal Society resolved on a major expedition of about four years duration, so that the sea bed could be methodically explored. The Admiralty offered HMS Challenger, a wooden three masted ship with a 1234 horsepower engine driving a single propeller. She was of a class known as a steam corvette and had a displacement of 2306 tons and was about fourteen years old at the time of the expedition. All but two of her 64 pounder main deck guns were removed and she was extensively rebuilt with a laboratory, dark room, aquarium, and large chart room, together with cabins for the many scientists.

In her three-and-a-half-year voyage she travelled over 68,000 miles, sailing part of the time and using her engine at others and when trawling, dredging, or taking soundings. She collected mineral as well as botanical and zoological specimens and made extensive deep sea soundings, temperature readings and analyses of the chemical composition of sea-water samples. She not only laid the basis for the present science of oceanography but she collected so much data that it is still being studied today.

Left *An impression dated about 1900, of HMS Beagle. She was a 90 foot three master, classed as a ten gun brig of 242 tons.*

Below *HMS Challenger, a wooden three master with a 1234 horsepower engine, driving a single propeller. She was a steam corvette.*

Chapter V
The fighting ships

Sea battles were at first not much more than sea-going extensions of similar contests ashore. The ambition of each ship commander was to get close alongside his opponent and to have a go, man to man, with bows and arrows, slings, and spears. Just such a battle is shown on the tomb of Ramses III, with the Egyptians and a tribe from the north going at it hammer and tongs. In the same manner the early warships were ordinary vessels which had been taken over for military use. They were manoeuvred in battle in the Mediterranean, almost entirely by oars and it is true to say that no battle ever took place or was able to take place in anything other than very settled conditions. As the centuries slid past, the emphasis on galley fighting power concentrated as much on the power plant and its drilled manoeuvrability as it did on the quality of the fighting men embarked. Speed to outrun your opponent was of course important, but so also was great skill in boat handling. In galley fighting it was possible to crush an enemy in one quick manoeuvre which might be anything from an outright ramming to a turn which would sweep away a whole bank of oars. The battle of Salamis in 480 BC was dominated by the trireme but very little evidence is left to give us a clear picture of this outstanding war boat.

Ships were built of wood and fabric and coated with tar and paint and other combustibles and seamen were rightly more scared of fire than almost any other danger afloat. Fire was therefore an obvious early nastiness to add to the armoury. For instance, the sailors of Rhodes in the third century BC made great use of fire buckets stuck out on the ends of poles. In fact, fire was as decisive a weapon at Actium as it was against the Spanish Armada. The Byzantine Romans went even further with the perfection of Greek fire, which some say was a type of liquid bitumen blown out by means of large bellows through copper tubes, to spray in a jet of flame for some distance. The main Roman contribution, however, followed the main desire for a good stand up fight. They invented the grappling hook and other devices to catch and hold the enemy craft steady and close while the soldiers got to work on each other.

In Northern Europe the same style of sea-fighting, man to man, in side by side combat, persisted right up until the development of the gun. The Norsemen may have had special war vessels but they were more designed for raiding other shore establishments, than for any special advantage in a ship to ship contact. Warships and merchantmen were generally interchangeable until the beginning of the sixteenth century. Henry III, for instance, used to lease his warships for merchant voyages and other kings hired merchant ships as they were required for war. Henry V built a special navy of 35 ships of superior size including the *Grace Dieu* built in 1418. She is recorded as being fitted with one great mast, one mizzen, two bowsprits, six sails and eleven bonnets (extra sails) but this is probably an inventory which included spares.

At the beginning of the sixteenth century, guns were made rather like barrels by welding iron bars together into a tube form and then securing them with iron hoops. Such guns were in effect breech loading which added to the general danger and modest power, although they were built up to eight inch bore and the firing of a 68 lb shot. The introduction of muzzle loaders, cast of brass in one piece and bored out with some accuracy, changed the picture for naval gunnery with increased range and accuracy. At the same time it changed the whole picture of naval warfare and warship design. By the death of Henry VIII guns had been standardised in a range of sizes from 3 to 32 pounders, which persisted throughout the life of the sailing warship.

The first cannons were placed in the forward and after castles and on the open deck, but as they became heavier and indeed, as the castles became loftier there came an urgent need to get the weight lower in the ship. A Frenchman, Descharges of Brest, is credited with the revolutionary idea of cutting the actual hull sides for gunports. To boat-builders it must have sounded heretical, since for centuries their efforts had been given to maintaining structural strength and to making the planking impregnable. However, no doubt despite their protests, gunports were in general use for warships by 1514. The *Henry Grace a Dieu* for instance carried a number of guns on the lower deck, with their muzzles appearing through ship-side ports. When she was rebuilt, in 1540, she reappeared with two rows of guns under the open deck. When she first came out she was fitted with no less than 186 guns, but these were later reduced to 122, probably of greater power. The cast cannons were extremely heavy. It is noted that the *Mary Rose,* for instance, carried brass 18 pounders which weighed two tons each.

Henry VIII established a British navy on a permanent basis and kept extensive records. The ships of Henry VII were carrack built with a poop and on bigger ships an additional poop royal. Henry VIII inaugurated several changes, of which the most important was the change to carvel planking. Clincher planking is difficult to repair once it has been strained and it is essentially a light construction. It seems possible that the powerful new cannons were too much for it and carvel construction became the norm for all future northern warships. Henry VIII also had the sterns cut off in a square transom style, which apart from being easier to construct, also allowed guns to be placed in a position so that they were pointing astern for chases.

The Henry Grace a Dieu also carried a very extensively extended rig, probably arranged as much for show as for any practical reasons. She carried topgallant masts at the head of her fore and main masts and flew topsails and topgallant sails on them. Her lateen mizzen sported its own lateen topsail and even a lateen topgallant, while an additional mast, the bonaventure mizzen, carried a lateen and a lateen topsail. It must surely have been a display of extravagance for many of her sails could have been of little value to her propulsion. Big ships, however, may have been necessary for national prestige, for a Portuguese vessel of the same period is said to have carried 140 guns and to

Left Galleys at the battle of Salamis, fought between the Greeks and the Persians. As a result of Themistocles' foresight, the Greeks though outnumbered, drove off the Persian navy.

Below The use of flame-throwers in ship to ship combat was an effective means of disarming an assailant, provided the attacking ship could get close enough.

Below right A 16th century woodcut showing galleons exchanging broadsides. The sternpost rudder shown on the ship on the left is worthy of note.

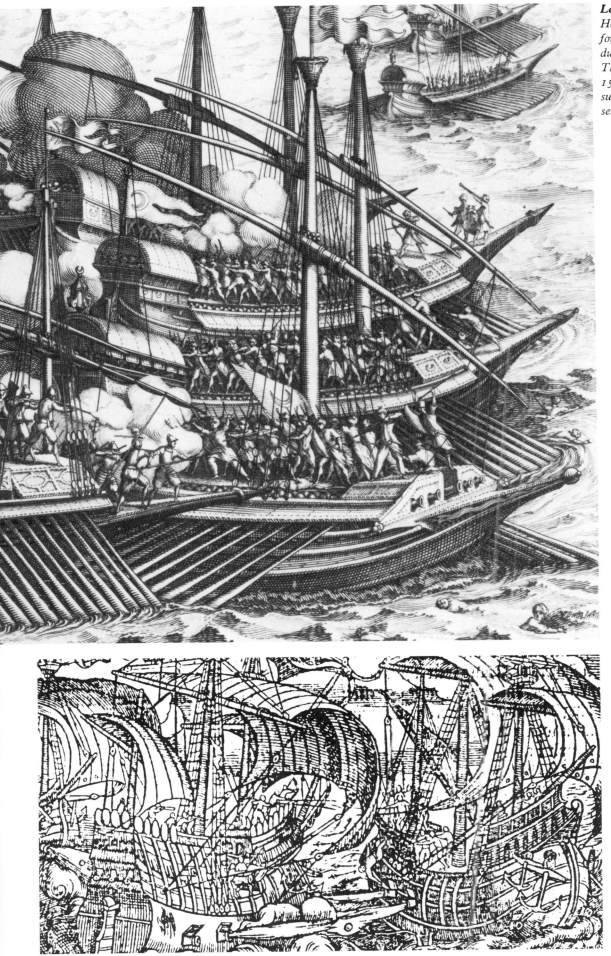

Left *The Knights Hospitallers were famous for their conquests at sea, during the 16th century. They were given Malta in 1530 and achieved great success in the Turkish seige of 1565.*

85

Right The Henry
Grace a Dieu or Great
Harry was built in 1500
for Henry VIII. She
carried an extended rig,
probably arranged both
for show and practical
purposes and topgallant
masts at the head of her
fore and main masts, in
addition to other
extravagances.

Vol. VI. Pl. XXII. p.208.

Tunnage.....1000.

MEN
Soldiers..........349
Mariners........301 }700
Gunners..........50

Right Henry VIII
inaugurated several
changes in the
construction of ships.
The most important was
the change from clincher
planking to carvel
planking. He also had
the sterns cut off in a
square transom style,
which was easier to
construct and allowed
guns to be placed
astern for chases. This
illustration depicts the
embarkation of Henry
at Dover.

Vol. VI. Pl. XXII. p.208.

Left The Ark Royal. The English fighting ships of the 16th century were superior to all others of the time because the English appreciated the potentialities of marine gunners. During this period, the English cut down the castles, which had been intended for boarding in close combat and improved the manoeuvrability in action.

have had, like the Henry Grace a Dieu, no less than six decks.

The next dominant warship type, is undoubtedly the galleon. The origins of the type are obscure but the galleon seems to have appeared as the result of a desire for more speed. It is possible that the galley was known to be a fast vessel and therefore the galleon was an attempt to make a sailing ship with galley-like proportions of hull. Certainly the galley was a much slimmer vessel. Another possible connection lies in the manner in which the galleon has the forecastle set back, often behind the foremast, to leave a long beakhead forward which might have appeared to bear some similarity to the ram of a galley. The galleon is thought of as a Spanish type. It may well have started there, but it spread in a few years right through Europe. By 1588 it is said that English galleons were the best and in fact all naval ships right up to Nelson's day were technically galleons.

The reason why the English galleons were superior to the native born Spanish ships, when the Armada was defeated in 1588, lay in the appreciation by the English of the potentialities of marine gunners. The English ships had greatly cut down the high castles which were after all intended to give a commanding platform when boarding. Unless ships are locked together, the high castles are no better than an improved target area and are a liability in manoeuvring the ship, especially in a breeze.

Elizabethan ships were still constructed with a high sheer, but the high deckworks were replaced, with what we can properly call a quarter deck and a poop. The interior decks had no relation to the

Below A Spanish galleas carried soldiers for boarding parties and hand to hand combat, as well as sailors. The broadside guns were mounted below a tier of oars, which had to be raised so that the weapons could be fired without the vessel crippling herself.

sheer but were planned as best suited the accommodation, holds and gun batteries.

Most galleons had three masts but many of the bigger ones sported a somewhat ineffectual fourth mast, in the form of a tiny lateen stuck right at the end of the poop. Ten of the English ships at the Armada battle were rigged in this manner, although it is more likely that they were principally rigged for show in much the same way that the Victorians added dummy funnels to their steamships to demonstrate power and speed. In any case the fourth mast persisted up until the middle of the seventeenth century, when at the time of James I it quietly departed from the scene. More important, a method of lowering, or striking, the topmasts at sea was suggested to the English navy soon after

1578. This offered additional security at sea in very bad weather and obviously led to experiment with bigger sail plans and even to carrying canvas longer as the wind piped up. This additional sail power may well have been yet another nail in the coffin of the ill fated Armada.

It is about this time, that the hitherto, closely guarded family secrets of ship design were being written down and brought into the open. A treatise by Matthew Baker compares the underwater lines to those of a fish and Sir Walter Raleigh himself is found offering the advice that, the best proportions for a warship in effect define a ship of about 140 feet in length overall, and with a beam of about 35 feet. Other aspects of Elizabethan design included the introduction of quarter galleries, which were used principally as latrines for the after cabins. These galleries were an obvious feature of the vessel and became one of the focal points for the elaborate decorations which became prevalent. Galleries were also built across the stern, but they were very vulnerable and together with the quarter galleries eventually became enclosed and glazed.

The use of transom sterns with overhanging aft castles, meant that the tiller disappeared inside the ship where it was controlled by a helmsman, who responded to orders passed down to him from the deck. In a ship of any size the tiller would be an enormous and deadly piece of wood which would be controlled by tackles worked in bad weather, by teams of sailors. The Elizabethans connected the ends of the steering tackles together and to a small vertical tiller mounted forward of the main tillers, called a whipstaff. This gave very fine control, although with a very restricted rudder movement; however, it did mean that it could be placed where the helmsman could stick his head through a hole in the deck for direct receipt of his orders and for a proper sight of the sails. Obviously major changes of the ship's direction were carried out by backing and filling the sails and, in bad weather, extra hands on the 'relieving' tackles to the tiller would still be required.

Warship development in the Mediterranean through this period still followed the use of rowing

The winds were too fresh or light to manoeuvre heavy fighting ships

powered vessels. The winds were either too fresh or too light for heavy sailing ships to be manoeuvred easily into fighting contact and this is the main reason why, for instance, the pirate galleys were so successful. Sails were fitted for whatever use they might be, but essentially the ships were designed for use under power and the battle tactics depended on the use of that power.

Right up to the middle of the fourteenth century, it seems likely that the galleys were generally arranged with the oars in two banks, one placed more or less above the other. At the end of the century a new style appeared, with the oars arranged in pairs side by side and at the end of the century, these were increased to work in groups of three. In rig they were usually fitted with two or three masts and in at least one picture, the centre sail is shown as a squaresail. A Venetian galley builder produced a manual for the guidance of other galley builders and noted down the standard sizes. These ranged from a Fusta of about 88 feet in length with 13 foot beam, to a galley of 151 feet in length and over 24 feet wide. The smallest is given a depth of four-

Below A plan of an English galleon. It was faster and more manoeuvrable than the unwieldy Spanish galleon, and had powerful long range guns. It was ships like this that were to defeat the Spanish Armada and establish English domination of the oceans of the world.

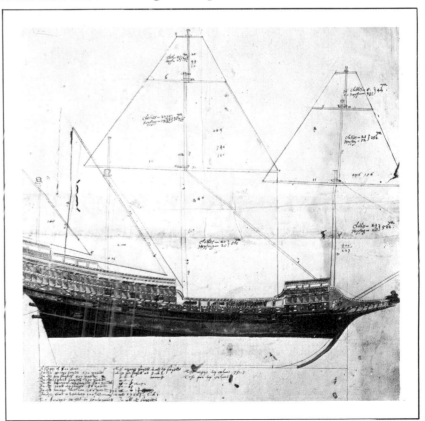

89

and-a-half-feet and the largest of 10 feet.

The most decisive and greatest galley fight ever fought was the battle of Lepanto in 1571. 273 Turkish ships were defeated by the combined fleets of Spain, Venice, Genoa, Malta, and the Pope, totalling 208 ships. A deciding feature of the Christian fleet was the use of galleasses, designed by the Venetian, Francesco Bressano. These high sided heavy ships, attempted to combine the advantages of the galley in rowing manoeuvrability and independence from the wind, with greatly increased sail area and much greater gun power. The ornamental point of the galley was replaced by a portable metal ram, but their principal offensive weapons

were the guns which were mounted in structures built forward and aft. The rowers were also partly protected by an upper fighting deck which ran between the forward and after castle over their heads and some further guns were spaced along this deck.

A hundred years later the Mediterranean galleass

Above *The Spanish galleass combined the speed of the galley and the striking power of the galleon, which was the battleship of the 16th century, designed specifically for war. It was longer in proportion to its beam than the greatships or armed merchantmen, which were primarily intended for commerce.*

Within the illustration:
DIEU · ET · MON · DROIT

Publish'd by John Pine, June 24, 1739, according to Act of Parliament.

Above *A souvenir print of the Spanish Armada, formed in its awesome defensive crescent, under attack by the English fleet.*

had not developed to any great extent. The ram, always an impractical weapon on such a cumbersome ship had disappeared, but the armament had not really increased. The problem was that, except at the ends, the heavy guns could not be placed low enough in the hull for the necessary stability, without getting in the way of the oars. A typical ship might be 160 feet long and propelled by 300 to 350 oarsmen. This demonstrates another weakness; any disturbance of the rowing pattern as might be caused by a single cannon ball landing among the rowers, would cause incredible chaos and cripple the whole ship in an instant. The sailing ship on the other hand can be fought and manoeuvred while there is a single spar with a sail on it left.

Seventeenth century galleys were divided into two main sizes, those with about 26 pairs of rowing benches and those which were larger and might have as many as 33 pairs. Each rowing bench would normally be occupied by as many as five men

giving a manpower requirement of 330 for a large ship, before the actual fighting men were counted. The colossal supply and logistics problems involved in running such war vessels limited their cruising range and general effectiveness still further.

In an attempt to employ bigger guns on board, the galleasses became larger and a reale, the ship of a king and therefore probably the best of its kind, from the end of the seventeenth century, might be 180 feet in length and about 21 feet in beam with a crew of 420 oarsmen. She would also have a pair of huge lateen sails of about 4,000 square feet each and the biggest gun would be a 36 pounder mounted low on the centreline and pointing over the bows. In order to aim this gun, the whole ship had to be conned. The whole concept was too vulnerable and we find a 26 gun frigate, the *Lion Couronne,* fighting off eleven galleys in 1651. In 1684 a single sailing ship defeated no less than 35 galleys. In fact the last battle in which the galley was actively employed

Above An 18th century print of the English men of war. The outstanding event of King George II's war with France was England's capture of Louisburg in 1745.

Below *This picture shows one of the many techniques developed for close combat in fighting ships. The use of fire could seriously debilitate the enemy.*

was the battle of Matapan in 1717.

Not a great deal of development occurred in European warships during the seventeenth century, although with records being kept, it was much better controlled. In British warships the straight transom stern was replaced with a curved tuck, which continued the main hull planking. This was a distinctive feature which marked them from others for many years. Charles I ordered the construction of an enormous warship, called appropriately

enough, the *Sovereign of the Seas*. Her length of keel was 127 feet and she had a displacement of 1,600 tons and cost ten times as much as any normal warship of the time. Originally she was finished with three decks of guns and a very great deal of gilt decoration, and the Dutch, against whom she was principally aimed, named her the *Golden Devil*. Pepys notes in his diaries, that he and some friends, managed to accommodate themselves inside her poop lantern.

The Sovereign of the Seas required a large sail area to drive her and to this end had another set of square topsails on her fore and aft masts. Later in her life, after the Restoration, she was renamed the *Royal Sovereign* and it is thought that the commonly used name of Royals for these sails comes from her original use of them.

The French, in reply to this enormous warship, built a vessel, *La Couronne,* of about the same dimensions but with only two decks and 72 guns.

As the lowest tier of guns could therefore be higher from the waterline, she was probably a better open water fighting proposition. In fact the Sovereign was later cut down to a two decker. The French navy fell into disuse until the 1660s, when Colbert ordered a sample set of Dutch warships to copy and set the French warship builders on a successful path. The Dutch at that time, no doubt with their shoal waters in mind, preferred two deckers of rather shallow draft.

Below *The most decisive and greatest galley fight ever fought, the battle of Lepanto in 1571. 273 Turkish ships were defeated by the combined fleets of Spain, Venice, Genoa, Malta and the Pope, totalling 208 ships.*

Above The bow, stern and quarter of the Sovereign of the Seas, later re-named the Royal Sovereign. Built for Charles 1, her keel was 127 feet and she had a displacement of 1600 tons.

Right Another view of the warship Royal Sovereign. She required a large sail area to drive her and therefore had an extra set of square sails on her fore and aft mast. It is thought that the name Royals, commonly given to these sails, comes from her use of them.

Right A pirate ship. The galley could be used both for stealth and speed, and this was the ship commonly chosen by pirates of this period.

Far right Admiral Nelson's flagship HMS Victory, sailing into action on October 21st 1805, off Cape Trafalgar.

At the beginning of the seventeenth century we begin to hear of frigates as a type of warship. Originally they seem to have been small, swift craft, armed with half a dozen or so guns but the size of ship grew with the appreciation of their qualities and it is not unusual to read of frigates with over 60 guns before the century was out. Essentially, however, the name frigate refers to a fast warship with a single gun deck.

Right up until the middle of the seventeenth century, warships fought together as seemed appropriate to the individual commanders. In 1653 the British Admiralty gave orders for ships to be fought in lines, so that their principal weapon, the broadside, could be fully effective. At the same time ships were divided into groups or rates, so that they could form up in these lines with others of approximately the same speed and seaworthiness. The definitions of the rates varied as time went on but a very rough guide, would give first rates over 90 guns, second rates over 80 guns, third rates over 50 guns, fourth rates over 38 guns, fifth rates over 18 guns, and sixth rates over 6 guns. These classifications came into normal usage in other navies. The first three rates were considered strong enough to fight in the battle line and were thereafter known as ships of the line.

Eighteenth century British warships were tightly controlled by the Admiralty and ships were built strictly to approved models and controlled dimensions, the so-called 'establishment ships'. The design advances, which came from the top during this period, tended to be concerned with the re-organization of guns, so that they were fewer in number but bigger in power. Hull design advances came almost exclusively from careful examination of captured French and other ships, whose builders had been more free to experiment. However, improvements were usually incorporated in the British ships once they were proven and the breed was continually developed in detail by extensive sea use. Anson, for instance, on his return from his round the world voyage in *Centurion* added his recommendations for fewer but larger guns and also that the channels or chains which held the

shrouds outside the hull should be raised a deck where possible, to keep the ship drier in rough water.

Decoration became more severe with this increased emphasis on seakeeping and practical changes occurred in the rig. The mizzen started the eighteenth century as a lateen sail but soon the fore part was cut away, when it was found to be doing little actual work. The useless end of spar followed it and the sail replaced by the gaff sail

By the end of the 18th century, the mizzen was a large, important sail

commonly found in small craft. This sail became called the spanker in merchant ships and the driver in warships.

By the end of the century it became a large and important sail fitted with a boom. The jib or staysail was in use in small ships as early as the beginning of the sixteenth century, but the introduction into square rigged ships was an important step which occurred in the middle of the eighteenth. It had two main advantages. Together with the driver a full outfit of staysails added materially to the windward capabilities of the ships, which had been considerably eroded by the extensive rigging necessary to hold up their enormous sail plans. This rigging

prevented the yards being braced round far enough and also presented enormous windage drag, which added to the leeward drift when the ships were on the wind. Also, again coupled with the driver, the fore and aft sails made for very easily handled manoeuvring sails. A backed jib would give a considerable turning moment to help a ship onto a new course or when manoeuvring in harbour. The bowsprit grew to match the new headsails and sprouted jib booms and flying jib booms, all of which had to be supported by rigging, producing extensive systems of bowsprit shrouds and martingales.

By the end of the eighteenth century, in time for Nelson's famous sea battles, the square rigger was complete in every essential detail and the sailing warship had reached her ultimate perfection. Nelson's perfect understanding of sea war under sail and his confidence in breaking the strict line orders at Trafalgar, which had held for a hundred and fifty years, was matched by a well trained, experienced fleet of ships, which were above everything else, reliable in their performance.

The *Victory* herself was an old ship at Trafalgar, having been built in about 1760. She was twice rebuilt before the battle, with the open galleries in her stern closed in and the channels moved up, in line with Anson's recommendations. Her total length is 226 feet and her maximum beam 51 feet. At

Below One of the biggest and best frigates ever built, The Constitution, shown in this oil painting by Birch with the Guerrier. Built in the 1790's, she was one of a fleet of six.

Trafalgar she was armed with 102 guns, ranging from 32 pounders on the lower deck, to 12 pounders on the forecastle deck. She also had a pair of 68 pounder carronades and she was fought at Trafalgar by a crew of 850 men. She was a representative of a class of nominally 110 gun first rates, which was planned in

United States, Constitution, President – The biggest frigates built

the middle of the eighteenth century. The great majority of warships were, however, 74 gunners, which perhaps was the most popular and effective size.

The biggest and best frigates ever built, are said to be the six American ships built in the 1790s. The *United States, Constitution,* and the *President* were about 204 feet in length (twenty feet longer than any other frigates) and 44 feet beam. They were officially rated as 44 gun ships, although they probably carried as many as 50 guns. The President is noted for carrying a fantastic cloud of sail, including royals and skysails, and the Constitution was said to have been able to make over thirteen knots in a good wind.

The last major battle fought wholly under sail was in 1827 at Navarino Bay, when the French, English and Russians combined to strike a blow for Greek independence. Admiral Codrington, fought a four hour battle in the *Asia,* 84 guns, together with 26 other ships, to defeat the sizeable Turkish fleet anchored in a crescent in Navarino Bay, at the very southern tip of Greece. The Turkish fleet was annihilated and it is said that only one Turkish ship, a frigate, escaped serious damage.

Following Trafalgar and right up until the finish of the sailing warships, they remained essentially the same, particularly in hull form, although the appearance underwent some changes. In 1811 the Admiralty finally abolished the beakhead bulkhead, a somewhat vulnerable piece of structure dating back to the galleons, and replaced it with the round bow, built right up to forecastle level. This was a very practical improvement and made ships very much drier when working in a seaway, while improving the forward firing arcs of the bow chasers. A similar improvement was tried aft and the whole stern gallery was replaced with a round stern, on which guns were mounted pointing aft. This was so monumentally ugly that it was quickly replaced by the elliptical stern. Bulwarks were built up solid and the last vestiges of the old open deck disappeared, as the forecastle was extended to join the quarterdeck, structurally at any rate. The last of the pure sailing warships were not beautiful and the ships look in their portraits, as if they were uncomfortably waiting for the cataclysmic change to steam propulsion.

Below HMS Asia, one of the ships with which Admiral Codrington fought the last battle under sail. The British fleet of 27 ships defeated the Turks at Navarino Bay in 1827.

Below *This 19th century print depicts the departure of the Honourable East India Company's ship Inglis, from St. Helena in company with other vessels.*

Chapter VI
The traders and the clippers

The ordinary everyday merchantman usually gets scant attention from the artists and the chroniclers, especially if there is some dramatic contest such as a war going on. This helps make it difficult for us to realize the considerable number of ships that were in daily use in the sixteenth and seventeenth centuries. At the beginning of the seventeenth, however, it is recorded that the Dutch, the dominant sea trading nation of the time, had over ten thousand ships, manned by a hundred thousand or so seamen.

The principal ship type was the *fluyt*, a rather flat bottomed, narrow ship with a rounded stern. Apparently the early craft of the type were heavily influenced by the prevailing method of assessing

Nova Britannia.

OFFERING MOST

Excellent fruites by Planting in
Virginia.

Exciting all such as be well affected
to further the same.

LONDON
Printed for Samvel Macham, and are to be sold at
his Shop in Pauls Church-yard, at the
Signe of the Bul-head.
1609.

Above *An advertisment of 1609 for emigrant ships shows the great increase in social mobility during the 17th century which was brought about by the developments in sail. This example offers most excellent opportunities for planting in Virginia.*

Above right *A 17th century oil painting of a Dutch East Indiaman, near the shore. The merchant ships rapidly became streamlined for a quick safe passage to the Indies.*

Right *Dutch East Indiaman about to engage in battle. Since they had to fight off pirates and were occasionally used in the colonial wars, the ships were very similar to naval frigates in construction.*

tonnage for dues and were excessively narrow on the deck. A new system of measurement became current about 1669 and later ships were less exaggerated. It seems that later the *fluyt* developed into the *pink*, still showing the rounded stern, but with a stern castle projection which was greatly narrowed (possibly pinked) in at the after end. A *pinnace* was thought to be a smaller version of the *fluyt*, but with a transom rather than a planked stern. The *fluyt* was apparently rigged, with three masts with squaresails and topsails on both the forward masts and a lateen mizzen. Topgallants

Merchantmen were armed like warships throughout the 18th century

were occasionally fitted but they were normally omitted to make the ships easier to handle, a desirable factor with the general shortage of seamen for such a large Dutch fleet.

In fact all manner of rigs are to be seen in contemporary illustrations. At the time ships were more commonly categorized by their hull type, or the use to which they were put, rather than by their rigs. Identification by rig came later, probably with the vast increase in ocean going which took place in the nineteenth century. When the hull is over the horizon, it makes better sense to recognize a ship by the sail plan which is visible. Names like *polacca* and *barque* turn up in contemporary documents. *Polacca* is generally meant to imply that the ship is rigged with pole masts in one piece rather than in separate lower, topmasts and topgallant masts, which were necessary in the bigger ships and warships. *Barque*, however, seems to mean quite different things to different writers and is not necessarily connected with the barque rig of the clipper ship times.

The Swedish master shipwright Chapman, in a book published in 1768, divides merchant ships into five types: the *frigate* which was flat sterned, the *hagboat* where the stern planking continued up to the taffrail at the top of the hull, the *pink* with its rounded and narrowed stern, the *cat* and the *barque*. The first three groups were fitted with beakheads, the latter two were not.

Throughout the eighteenth century the majority of merchantmen were armed. Thus they looked very like warships except that on closer inspection it could be seen that they carried fewer guns, or guns of lesser power. The normal rig was that of the frigate, but some owners refused to fit topgallants, whereas others gave their ships the full outfit up to and including royals.

The original *East Indiamen* were small roomy vessels probably of the pinnace type but rigged and fitted out in a manner very similar to naval frigates. This was as a result of both fear of pirates on their route to the Indies and of their occasional employment in colonial wars. Throughout the life of the East India companies, the size of their ships grew. Chapman, for instance, shows a ship of 676 tons pierced for 28 guns and obviously based on the 32 gun class frigates. By the end of the century the East Indiamen were 1,200 tonners, based largely

Right *This 19th century painting shows shipping in the Thames estuary.*

Opposite *The Old Custom House Quay, shown in this painting by Samuel Scott (1702-1772). Pictured are mid-18th century vessels.*

on 64 gun warships, although with a need for greater cargo volume they had flatter floors and fuller bilges. Steel's 'Naval Architecture' of 1804 details a 1,257 ton East Indiaman which again is very like a large sailing warship to the casual observer but with important differences on closer inspection. The upper deck is continuous, with a very flat sheer, the shipsides are wall-like and without the tumblehome of the warship and the bilges are fuller for cargo capacity. Most important however the bottom row of gunports are just painted on the outside and the lower deck is not pierced at all for guns. By 1815 high bulwarks were fitted from end to end and the

Of a fleet of 200 coasters, 140 were wrecked off the Norfolk Coast

East Indiamen lost all appearance of the gracefully curved sheer which had been a mark of the sailing ship since the time of reed rafts.

Throughout their joint history, the *West Indiaman* was always a very much smaller ship than the East Indiaman, scarcely reaching 800 tons in size and usually nearer 500. Although the West Indiaman carried guns and were rigged along warship lines, they looked very different. In place of the rather smooth profile of the warship and contemporary merchant ship, they showed a very irregular outline with as many as four different deck levels. For some reason they followed the Elizabethan builder in putting headroom below decks, were it suited the accommodation requirements rather than the other way around. Such a vessel might have eight guns a side, but these would appear through the shipside on four different levels. Eventually, the West Indiaman was tidied up to look a bit more like a small frigate but never approached anything like the full line of battle majesty of the East Indiaman.

By this time the main trade routes were established around the world, with merchant ships sticking as far as possible to paths which gave them the maximum amount of fair wind sailing. In the Trade winds for instance, and the minimum of both head winds and calms. When it came to working into harbour, they would if there were any baffling breezes, sit tight until the wind changed, in their favour or, latterly, until a steam tug arrived. Small craft were never important enough for tugs and in Europe and North America had to work in tidal streams and currents which might equal their maximum sailing speeds. Windward performance therefore was of much greater moment to them than it was to the big ships. If it is difficult to grasp the sheer numbers of offshore craft, it is much more so to realise how many small craft there were or generally, how dangerous their work was. In 1692 one hundred and forty of a fleet of two hundred coasters were reported wrecked on the north Norfolk coast, together with fifty ships outward bound from the Wash. In 1755 a fleet of over two hundred coasters was reported putting out of Yarmouth Roads, for the north and running into trouble. In 1770 thirty vessels are reported cast up on Lowestoft sands, and so the reports can be read until this century.

Most of the small coasters probably were rigged with two masts and the name brigantine starts to be seen at the end of the seventeenth century for two masted vessels square rigged on both masts. When the name *brig* began to be commonly used for this rig, the definition of a *brigantine* became one of a square rig on the foremast and fore and aft rig on the mainmast. There were of course all manner of variations, including the snow rig where a third mast was set up immediately aft of the mainmast, specifically to let the gaff sail operate clear of all the gear on the mainmast. Basically it was a means of fitting a bigger gaff sail, or spanker as it was known in three masters, without altering the proportions of the brig rig.

The French channel fisherman developed from the time of the middle ages the lugsail rig, which is a square rig turned on its side to operate closely fore and aft. The French lugger often had three masts and fitted topsails over each lower sail and added a jib working on a long bowsprit for good measure. As a windward rig it is excellent although difficult or troublesome to tack. This rig emphasizes again the importance of windward ability to the small boat working in open water, which might have to make over the wind and tide to get home.

The gaff rigged cutter was generally used by the English and other European nations as a despatch and patrol vessel. The rig seems to have stemmed from the rig the Dutch used for their yachts, which were developed from small fast patrol craft. A gaff cutter of the eighteenth century would have a gaff

Opposite *The famous American Bluenose Schooner. These fast sailing ships were developed in response to the need for speed in the race for the riches of the New World, which was open to the fastest traders afloat.*

mainsail, a staysail and a jib or bowsprit staysail and would have a squaresail as a running sail. Some cutters used upper and lower square topsails and presented a very lofty appearance.

There is an apocryphal story, that when a small two masted vessel was launched at Gloucester, Massachusetts in 1713, she entered the water so gracefully that her owner was moved to comment on how well she 'schooned' thereby inventing the whole breed of *schooners*. Two masted fore and aft rigged craft had certainly been seen before, among the general array of rigs in Europe and possibly also in America. However, there is no doubt that the American schooner became a distinct and extremely successful type of craft in its own right. It may have been promoted by the generally offshore winds of the east coast of America, which put a premium on fast sailing with the wind abeam. The Admiralty in their careful way, recorded the lines

The American schooner became a successful ship in its own right

of an American schooner showing a craft with a distinct air of the caravel about her hull form and carrying a great deal of sail. She was two masted with gaff sails on each mast. The foremast is set well forward leaving no room for a staysail but she is fitted with two jibs on a long bowsprit and has square topsails on both masts.

In the 1830s, the fastest ships afloat were the *Blackwall frigates*. These ships were built on the Thames privately for charter to the East India Company but followed a very standardized form, so that they would be readily acceptable to the company. When their monopoly of the eastern trade was repealed in 1833, the way was open for improvements to be made. In 1838 the Blackwall yard built frigates which were without a poop and with only a single set of stern and quarter windows. A few years later the Smith yard on the Tyne launched a pair of ships, the *Marlborough* and the *Blenheim*, with completely flush decks.

Meanwhile the Americans had fully discovered the advantages of fast sailing ships, after successfully building ships for blockade running and privateering

Below *The Boston Tea Party. Unimpressed by the East India Company's desire to avoid bancruptcy by shipping surplus tea into America, patriotic Bostonians flung the chests into the harbour.*

Right *The Cutty Sark, perhaps the most famous of all sailing ships. This beautiful tea clipper was used for many years on the eastern run, bringing tea from China to London.*

Below *A model of the Thomas W Lawson. Built in 1902 she was the only seven masted schooner ever constructed. She was 395 feet in length, 50 feet beam and with a depth of hold of 35 feet. It was claimed that she had given the biggest cargo capacity ever carried by sail.*

Bottom *The opening of the Suez Canal in 1869 signalled the downfall of the tea clippers. This illustration shows a procession of ships in the canal in the transition from sail to steam. It was thought that the tea reached England in better condition in wooden ships, but the speed of the iron steamships was unbeatable.*

during the 1812/4 War of Independence. The same ships were put to peaceful uses after the war and were found to be in great commercial demand. They were in equal demand by pirates, smugglers, and slavers on the one hand and by the navies who had to catch them on the other. Baltimore-built ships had an excellent reputation for their performance and this thriving demand helped to develop a long hulled fine, even hollow bowed, type of vessel, which became known as the *Baltimore clipper*.

The transatlantic trade in the 1820s was a fairly leisurely one in terms of speed. A typical immigrant ship from Europe would probably take forty days for the voyage, possible not a matter of great importance to the first class passengers accommodated in cabins in the poop, but appalling for the main bulk of the immigrants who were packed into the 'tween decks like sardines. This profitable trade was wide open to take over by steam and a regular steamship service was in operation by 1838. Wild competition between the steam packets and sailing clipper packets went on for years, with the sailing ships being driven harder and harder to keep up with the reliable timing of the steamships. The sailing ship still remained supreme for longer passages, where the problems of coaling limited her rivals but the pressure was on all the time to push up the speed of these vital crossings.

By 1843 American shipbuilders had begun to apply the lessons learned in the Baltimore brigs and schooners to larger ships. They had begun to design and produce large full rigged sailing ships of 750 tons with the same style of hull. The first real clipper ship, as we understand the term, was probably the *Rainbow* launched at New York in 1845. She was revolutionary of course, in her fine hull after two centuries of wide bowed ships, but most startling to the eye must have been her stark simplicity. Painted black without any of the gunports and very little indeed of the giltwork, she must have looked extremely fast and elegant and she certainly proved both fast and commercial. 1847 saw the discovery of gold in California and started an almost insatiable demand for passages from the east coast, for would-be gold diggers round the Horn to the goldfields. Ship owners could almost charge what they liked for passage in a fast ship and they could sign up as many crew as they needed, who were only too pleased to work their passages to California. The demand for fast vessels was intense and limited entirely to American ships by American law. The problem lay in the accummulation of ships on the west coast as their crews lit out for the goldfields. Fortunately, this problem practically

Above The famous race home from China, between the Ariel and the Taeping. They arrived home within hours of each other after 98 days at sea. The Ariel was built in 1865 by Steele and Sons at Greenock.

111

Below *The five masted sailing ship HMS Agincourt, passes a lighthouse.*

coincided with the repeal of British Navigation Acts which had limited British trade to British ships. The clippers could now embark a double crew, lose half of them to the gold rush, sail for China to load tea, and make a profitable voyage to London. The slower British ships which had been keeping the tea trade to themselves, found that they were quite outclassed for the valuable first tea crop and had to be content with the unprofitable follow-up cargoes.

There had not really been a great demand for fast ships for the British trade until this point. The British equivalent of the Baltimore clippers were

The wood shortage led to the introduction of iron and steel

the small fast schooners and brigs which were built in Scotland, principally in Aberdeen, for the Baltic trade and of which the *Scottish Maid* of 1839 is probably the first with real clipper potential. The British started building clippers following the Americans and had a long hard struggle to catch up. After the building of the enormous fleets of wooden ships which culminated in Trafalgar, there was something of a shortage of wood in England suitable for shipbuilding. Therefore, there was a great deal of experiment with iron components, particularly knees and frames.

European shipbuilders pressed ahead with iron in ship construction, whereas the Americans with great reserves of timber stuck to wood construction. Steam ships came quite quickly to iron plating, but it was thought by seamen that the copper sheathing which was used to protect wooden ships from the shipworm of tropical waters, was essential to reduce fouling during a long passage. Copper sheathing on an iron ship presents frightening electrolytic corrosion problems and therefore the early English clippers were built of composite construction. That is with iron, and later steel, framing but planked with wood and sheathed with copper. Towards the end of the century, all sailing ships were built in iron; even the masts and spars were built of iron tubes and wire rigging had almost completely superseded rope for the standing rigging.

The California trade for clippers effectively came to a close when a railway was laid across the Isthmus of Panama, with connecting steamer services on both sides. Just as the demand for fast passages to California was dropping off, however, the Victoria gold rush started in Australia in the 1850s. The Americans were ready with fast and suitable ships, whereas the British ships were overwhelmed with would-be passengers. The American ships had increased in size, to 1,800 tons, while most English ships were less than half that size. Further, the American ships had a reputation for fast passages, making Atlantic crossings in about fourteen days west to east and eighteen days east to west; less than half the time of the old immigrant ships. American ships were leased to British owners and more ships were commissioned from American yards. McKay built the *Lightning* for a British owner in 1854, the

first ship to be built in the United States for a British owner since the War of Independence. The Lightning was 244 feet in length, by 44 feet beam and 1,468 tons. She was built with two complete decks and a poop extended forward for additional accommodation. She carried four cabins aft for first class passengers, housed the second class in a deckhouse amidships with twelve cabins, and the immigrants below decks.

The lines of the tea clippers of the 1850s and 60s were derived principally from the American wooden clippers such as the *Lightning* and *Champion of the Seas*, both designed by McKay. They were built with a beam to length ratio of about 5·5. The fully developed tea clippers such as the *Cutty Sark* and the *Thermopylae* were even finer with a ratio of about 5·7. They were also of rather finer section, for they were intended for a trade where the sheer bulk of the cargo was secondary to speed. There was a very large premium on the first of each season's tea crop to reach London. The tea clippers were probably the fastest ships ever produced, for they consistently outran the wool clippers when they were diverted to that trade. The Cutty Sark and the Thermopylae averaged 85 day passages from Melbourne to London over a decade, with a best run of 71 days, whereas the average for the genuine wool clippers over the same route was 90 days.

The British steel, wool clippers were very successful and it was in answer to their challenge that the American clipper master builder McKay built his masterpiece the *Great Republic* of 4 555 tons, 325 feet in length and 53 feet in beam. This marvellous ship carried a great spread of sail, as she was originally designed with skysails over her royals and moonsails over her skysails. She was square rigged on three of her four masts and fore and aft rigged on the fourth and would these days have been called a barque. In such a vessel sail handling had again become a problem for a working trading ship which could not carry unlimited hands who worked the rig on board warships. McKay split the topsails in the Great Republic in a manner which became standard for all ships in a few years. Sadly this ship caught fire before her maiden voyage in 1853 and although rebuilt, she was too late for her planned market and was not ever successful.

The Cutty Sark and the Thermopylae epitomise the tea clippers. They were both within a few feet of the same dimensions, which may not have been accidental, since the Cutty Sark was built as a rival to the other. They were not, however, outstandingly fast among tea clippers, although they both shone in the wool trade. The famous *Ariel*, for instance, was built in 1865 by Steele & Sons' yard at Greenock, who had by now rivalled the work of the original British clipper yards of Aberdeen. Their speciality was ships with very fine lines aft, which gave them additional ability to ghost along in calm weather. The Ariel in particular was said to be able to get along at four knots, by the shaking of her sails when all around her had stopped dead in the water. It is perhaps this ability, as much as top speed which made for the successful clipper. The ability to steal through a calm to the next patch

Left The five masted ship Preussen, built in 1902. She was 407 feet long and 53 feet in beam.

of wind, while your rival remained stuck in it could mean a large and profitable lead in a race to port. It was for this, as much as for speed with the wind blowing, that the clippers surrounded themselves with swathes of sail. The Ariel and the *Taeping* ran an epic race home from China one year, to arrive within hours of each other after 98 days. The Cutty Sark and the Thermopylae, although rated quite high as tea clippers never got within ten days of such a passage time.

The opening of the Suez Canal in 1869 effectively did for the tea clippers. Trade continued for a year or two, because the shippers thought that the tea would get home in better condition in wooden sailing ships rather than in iron steamers. When this did not prove to be the case, the 60 day passages via the canal by fast steamship were unbeatable and the tea clippers were put onto the Australian wool trade.

The later American wooden clippers were known as 'down easters', from the placing of the building yards of Maine, Massachusetts and Connecticut. They were built for capacity as much as for speed and were plainly constructed and finished without much decoration. The depression of 1868 effectively put an end to this construction and the very last wooden square rigger, the *Arvan*, was launched at Phippsburg in Maine in 1891.

Up until this time the average size of the wool clippers was about 2,000 tons but in the 1880s, in an attempt to increase efficiency and to keep costs down, they were built as large as 3,000 tons. At the same time, the use of iron construction had made the hulls some fifteen per cent lighter than wood and this gave additional cargo capacity. The wool clippers held their own in increasing competition until about 1890, when they were rebuilt and switched either to general cargoes or to the Chilean guano trade.

Somewhat forlorn attempts were made with even larger sailing ships to get the economics right and to make sailing ships pay again. In 1890 a steel five masted barque, the *France*, was launched from Hendersons yard in Glasgow for French owners. She was lost in 1901 but in 1902 the only five masted, full rigged ship ever built was launched. The *Preussen* was 407 feet long and 53 feet in beam. A second five masted barque, the *France II*, was built in France and launched at Rouen and was the largest sailing ship ever built. She was 8,000 tons, driven by a sail area of 68,350 square feet and was run by a crew of forty-five. She was, necessarily, fitted with every labour-saving device including two small auxiliary engines driving propellers. These were later removed and for a while the France II was a pure sailing vessel. During the first war, she was attacked by a German submarine, but escaped under a press of sail and with both motors running. She was lost in 1922 after going aground near the entrance to Noumea.

The American schooner builders also tried to get the economics right with increased size, for a time with success. Their answer was a large, simple hull propelled exclusively by fore and aft sails set on as many masts as necessary to get the required sail

Above This illustration gives some idea of the scale of these ships. It shows men on the yardarm.

Inset Members of the crew of the famous tea clipper the Cutty Sark.

area. Five and six masted schooners were common but the only seven masted schooner ever built was the *Thomas W. Lawson* in 1902. She was 395 feet in length, 50 feet beam, and with a depth of hold of 35 feet was claimed to have given the biggest cargo capacity ever carried by sail. It is interesting to compare her with the five masted square riggers, for in contrast to their forty-five man crews, the Thomas W. Lawson was run by a crew of sixteen. Unfortunately, after successful voyages off the American coast, she was sent across the Atlantic in 1907 and capsized off the Scillies. She was no beauty, but a brave attempt to keep sailing ships, in an increasingly mechanical age.

After the first world war, a number of sailing ships found employment in the Australian trade again but this time running wheat. It is sad to record that they were not so employed for their speed, or other advantages as ships, but because they were generally such a drug on the market that they could be kept as floating warehouses for their cargoes after they arrived. The commercial square rigger had effectively ended its days.

Steam had moved slowly at first into the maritime world. Seamen are probably more scared of fire at sea than of any other hazard. They took the utmost care over such matters as galley fires, which would be doused at the onset of any rough weather which might have rolled an ember or two onto the deck. To fit a roaring great boiler fire and a chimney, belching hot sparks into a wooden ship liberally coated with grease and tar, must have seemed the bad joke of all time. Further, to fill the cargo space with expensive coal for the ship's own boilers, rather than with paying cargo, must have looked like commercial suicide.

Steam power, actually produced successful propulsion for boats in the last quarter of the eighteenth century and was quickly accepted for such obvious

Above *The Sirius, a 100 ton steamer built for the Irish sea service. She was chartered in 1838 by the British and American Steam Navigation Company. The Sirius was one of the first steamers to be fitted with a surface condenser, instead of using salt water in the boilers.*

Right *The Savanah steamship. She was powered by paddle wheels.*

Copyright 1909 by Franz Hanfstaengl

119

uses as harbour tugs. But it was a long time before steam was trusted on its own for work offshore. The first steam engineed vessel to venture across an ocean in fact was the *American Savannah* in 1819, a fully rigged three master, which made occasional use of the engines. It was originally thought that the steam engine would form an auxiliary propulsion method for occasions when the wind did not serve, rather than the complete power unit it grew to be. The Savannah was powered by paddle wheels which, it is said, could be dismantled and stowed on deck in twenty minutes. Her modest smokestack had an elbow bend in it, so that it could be turned to improve the draught in the boiler.

The first Atlantic crossing with the steam engine working continuously the whole way, took place in 1838 when the 208 foot *Sirius* took 18 days and 10 hours between Cork and New York. Sirius was fitted with surface condensers, which allowed her boilers to be run all the way on fresh water, saving all the problems which had been found in attempting to use salt. The paddle steamer *Curacao* had previously actually steamed all the way from Rotterdam to Paramaribo in 28 days, but with frequent engine stops on the way for repairs to boilers and machinery. She was chiefly remarkable for her paddle wheels, which could be increased in diameter as the coal was used up and the ship floated lighter.

The strong mental division between the sailors and the engineers, is perhaps not surprising and persists up to the present day. The modern sailing yachtsman often resents the engine on which he relies for motoring to and from his moorings and there is a lack of real sympathy between the sailing men and the power cruisers. In the early days of steam, the seaman on deck clung to his masts and sails and even when his rig became much reduced persisted with high funnels, perhaps on the basis that if the worst came to the worst, a sail could be set on them. The engineers were just as blinkered, for their reports on early trials would often describe ship and engine in great detail and entirely ignore the lofty rig spread above them. Many of the pioneer craft were in fact delightful examples of what would be called motor sailers in these days. Patrick Miller's very early, twin hulled 25 foot steamer, was powered with a Symington atmospheric engine and had a two masted rig. It is recorded, that she made a good five knots under power, which would have been her speed under sail with a good breeze.

The building of iron ships, 'against nature' as it was to many seamen who could not see how they could float, must have been a great relief to seamen navigating the new steamships in continual fear of fire. The Atlantic is often taken as a proving ground for innovation and the legendary position of the *Great Britain*, the first screw propelled iron vessel to cross it, is not surprising. Designed by the master engineer of the day, Isambard Brunel, the 322 foot Great Britain was fitted with a thousand horsepower below decks, driving a six bladed, fifteen foot diameter propeller. Above decks, she had six rather short masts all fitted with gaff sails and best

described as schooner rigged, although she crossed square yards on two of them. Her first transatlantic voyage took under fifteen days at an average speed of over nine knots. She was very well built with six watertight compartments in her length and survived a year aground at Dundrum, use on the Australian run, conversion to sail, use as a hulk in the Falkland Islands and then neglect until she was recovered in 1970 and brought back to Bristol, where she was built, for restoration.

The general seafaring man's attitude to steam was however expressed by the Royal Yacht Squadron at a meeting in the Thatched House Tavern in 1827 in these terms:
'As a material object of this club is to promote seamanship and the improvements of sailing vessels, to

---

The beginnings of steam power were looked upon with distaste

---

which the application of steam engines is inimical, no vessel propelled by steam shall be admitted into the club and any member applying a steam engine to his yacht shall be disqualified thereby and cease to be a member'. Their attitude remained rigid until 1844 when the Squadron admitted yachts of more than 100 horsepower into membership, a view no doubt coloured by the building of the first Royal paddle steamer yacht, the *Victoria and Albert*, the year before.

The steam yacht then prospered and although most sailing men resisted the idea of putting machinery into their lovely craft, a good many appreciated the further freedom and seamanship of an auxiliary engine. Chief proponent of this approach was probably Lord Brassey, who had compound expansion engines of 350 indicated horsepower in his famous topsail schooner *Sunbeam*. In her he cruised great distances including a 37,000 mile, circumnavigation of the world. With her sails set, she looked like any of her sailing yacht contemporaries but when the wind dropped she could use her screw propeller to give her a speed of eight knots on four tons of coal a day.

This auxiliary engine approach looked attractive for the tea clippers and an experimental auxiliary steamer, the *Far East*, was built in the 60s. In order that her sailing performance should not be impaired the twin propellers could be lifted up into recesses in the stern. Whether this would have been a successful ship type or not is hard to say, for it was overtaken by the opening of the Suez Canal and the establishment of regular coaling depots all the way to China.

The ships of the conversion period from sail to steam were generally awkward looking craft and the auxiliary sail and the auxiliary engine sat together very uncomfortably. The problem was the sheer bulkiness of each power unit and although the principle of auxiliary propulsion was probably sound, there was not room on board for both. Now perhaps when powerful power units come in such very small packets we may see a revival of the auxiliary sailing ship.

Left This 19th century print shows the SS Great Britain in stormy seas. She was the first screw propelled iron vessel to cross the Atlantic.

Left The SS Great Britain, designed by Isambard Brunel, she was fitted with a 1000 horsepower engine below decks. She was recovered in 1970 and reconstructed in Bristol.

Chapter VII
Junks, dhows and others

The origins of boating in China and the far eastern world are much more difficult to trace than are those of the west. There is very much less evidence in literature or paintings and very much less in the way of grave goods and models. The Chinese in any case, went in for an extremely stylized manner of representing almost everything and this of course included their ships, so that they appeared to look the same for centuries whether or not this was the case.

The ruler Fu Hsi is supposed to have taught the Chinese the art of shipbuilding, at the same time as he taught them to fish in the year 2852 BC. There were written characters for the word boat and others for the action of propelling a boat with an oar and caulking the seams, in the time of the Shang

Below Dhows from the Arab world. They have many variations locally as a work boat but all types carry the lateen sail.

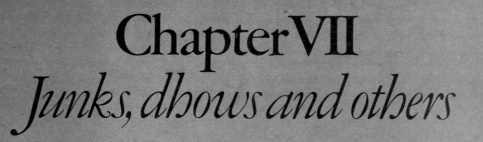

Above *Departure of Marco Polo from Venice. A variety of craft can be seen in the harbour.*

dynasty from 1766 to 1122 BC. However, it is generally agreed that the Chinese seagoing junks must be among the oldest known type of vessel and that their structural pattern may not have changed over a thousand years. The *Antung* trading junk, for instance, is thought to have been almost exactly the same last century as it was 2,500 years ago.

A civilization based around a river such as the Yangtze with its 2,000 miles of navigable waterway, could hardly have failed to have developed the ship at a very early stage in its progress. However, it was so remote from western civilisations that there was little contact before the Christian era, except

by way of the overland trade routes. One of the earliest recorded sea voyages by the Chinese is an invasion of Japan in 219 BC and it seems very likely that Chinese ships were trading with India by about the same time. These external contacts however produced very few paintings or written descriptions of the craft concerned. A description from the fifth century BC when China apparently started building ships for her seagoing trade described them as bull head ships. It seems likely that this may have been the ancester of the *Kiangsu* type of trading junk, also sometimes known as the *Pechili* trader. These large five masted junks traded north from the Yangtze making sea voyages of up to three weeks duration

Industriā res parvæ crescunt, socordiā magnæ 🙵 minuuntur.

Above left *Chinese junks at the time of Marco Polo. It is from the records of his voyages that we get the earliest detailed descriptions of the kinds of ships at sea at this time.*

Above right *Navigational instruments from the tomb of Robert Smith, 1697 in Waltham Abbey, Essex. Left a backstaff, top left, dividers and nocturnal cross staff (Jacob's staff) and, right, an hour glass.*

Left *A junk from the time of Magellan.*

in each direction. The biggest of them are thought to have been as long as 170 feet, although the greater number may have been half that length. In style they have a similarity to the caravel in profile, at first glance but the bow is really blunt and bull headed and the bottom is flat. The mainsail is rather square and set like a lugsail. Two similar but smaller sails, in descending order of size to the bow, lean progressively forward and the front mast is set right against the portside bulwarks to keep it clear of the mooring equipment. Aft there is a single sail set on the false transom with another tiny sail set between it and the main abreast of the tiller and also right up against the port bulwarks. The cabin accommodation is right aft, the full width of the deck and extending over the big barn door rudder which itself is partly concealed by the false transom. A stern gallery projects aft of this again, built on the bumpkins necessary to sheet the aftermost sail. A ship with some similarity to this is shown in a fresco found in caves at *Ajunta, Hyderabad* and dated to the fifth century AD, but it is far from distinct enough to be certain. In 417 AD a Buddhist monk, Fa Hsien, reported on a voyage from India to China. He mentioned that each ship carried about two hundred people and that the journey from Java to Canton which should have taken fifty days, actually took ninety; a complaint which will strike a chord

of sympathy with all travellers under sail. He also mentions more happily that behind each large ship was a smaller one to be used in case of disaster to the first one.

The Chinese are said to have invented many of the components and fittings used for western sailing vessels, including the centreboard, leeboards, the slotted perforated rudder, the windlass, and the use of watertight compartments. They are also credited by some with the invention of the compass, though this is disputed. The only clues we have are that they are said to have made use of direction finding chariots in 2697 BC and the earliest Chinese dictionary mention of the lodestone dated about 121 AD. Boatbuilders were mentioned about 1100 BC in the class of a hundred artisans and by 472 BC there is a record of a navy belonging to the Chinese state of Yueh. In 214 BC there is a reference to northern junks laden with iron being sunk to provide foundations for the Great Wall, and another milestone was passed in 132 BC when Chinese pirates were first mentioned in literature. The earliest detailed information about ships comes, however, from Marco Polo who set off for China in 1265 and who mentions seeing them in thousands during his travels. In particular he talks of a merchant ship with a single deck with no less than sixty small individual cabins for the merchants. The ship, he said, had four masts and two which could be set up and lowered again, one steering oar, and nine (some translations say twelve) sails. These ships were built of fir and spruce, double planked and caulked at each layer, with the planks fastened with iron nails. Such ships had, he said, watertight bulkheads, large ones as many as thirteen, in case the ship went on a reef or was damaged by whales which he mentioned as an occurrence which often happened. When repairs were needed and after the ship had seen a year of service the shipwrights would nail another layer of planks on top of those already there and caulk up the new lot. This went on year after year until she had six layers when she was considered no longer seaworthy and fit only for coastal voyaging.

The earliest European drawing of a junk is an illustration by the Dutchman H. Van Linschoten dating from 1596. This shows a suspiciously Dutch looking hull with junk like overtones including a

Left This early photograph (1870) by *J Thompson* shows a junk. The word junk is not a term the Chinese themselves use for their ships. It is probably derived from the Chinese word chu'an meaning boat or ship, via the Javanese djong, the Dutch jonk and the Portuguese junco.

very neatly rolled up sail hoisted at the main mast-head. The Chinese junk rig is one of the most ingenious and efficient ever devised and until comparatively recently was not really appreciated in Europe. Essentially it makes use of a quadrilateral sail set normally for use fore and aft much in a similar manner to the European lugsail which may be derived from it. The sail is however reinforced with full length battens at regular intervals up its height and each of these battens is secured to the mast, about a third of its length from forward, and controlled at its aft end by a complicated system of sheets. The sail gives a fairly balanced loading about the mast which cuts down the handling pressures in the sheets and the multiplicity of the latter reduces the strain on each part. When the halyard is let go, the sail gathers between a set of ropes stretching from the masthead to the boom and neatly stows itself. Furthermore, the sheeting arrangement is such that as it lowers, the bottom of the sail is gathered first. This allows the Chinese sailor extremely quick and easy adjustment of sail area, much faster than any reefing system developed in the west. The regular arrangement of battens takes a great deal of the strain off the cloth used for the sails and it is not uncommon to see a junk sailing happily at sea with sails which would be an unworkable disgrace in a western rig. It was this tattered aspect of the junk rig which brought it into poor regard when it was first seen by, for instance, the sailors of smart clipper ships.

There are many different types of junk and the term is not one which the Chinese themselves use for their ships. The word probably comes originally from the Chinese word *ch'uan* meaning boat or ship via the Javanese *djong*, the Dutch *jonk* and the Portuguese *junco*. The ships in China are classified more by district and the confusion and contradictions to any exact attempt to categorize them are many. One type which can be more or less readily identified perhaps is the *Foochow* pole or stock junks which were used in the timber trade from the rich forests of Fukien province in the south. These magnificent craft were large and seaworthy vessels which may have been as much as 180 feet in length with the narrow beam of about 28 feet. A beam length ratio of 6·4 compared with 5·7 of the extreme clippers in their prime. They were very strongly built with perhaps fifteen full depth bulkheads along the length of the hull. The shorter logs were stowed in the many deep holds formed by the bulkheads and the longer logs were carried both on deck and over the side lashed to the topsides. A raised quarter deck was built from just aft of amidships to the stern and the aft half of this was occupied by a large cabin. On top of this and concealed by the high and distinctive stern there might well be another small shelter compartment. The rudder, like many Chinese rudders, was both large and concealed inside the hull behind a false transom. The perforations helped to reduce steering loads and these could be further relieved by using the tackles provided, to lift the rudder bodily. The variable rudder area which was thus available may well have been necessary to give enough steering force for slow speed work manoeuvring in harbour, while at the same time only a small area would be necessary when such a large vessel was reaching fast up the coast at a maximum speed which might be up to sixteen knots.

The Foochow junk carried a fairly conventional three masted rig with each mast having a single sail

The many sailing communities developed distinct ship types

in the Chinese manner. The size of the masts is a little startling however for the mainmast of, for instance, a 140 foot junk has been quoted as being at least 120 feet high. This for a mast which was basically unstayed and bearing a sail which itself weighed several tons and which may have generated a thousand horsepower. Incidentally, it is thought that the Chinese junk which voyaged to England in 1848 and which was inspected by Queen Victoria was a Foochow junk, although probably specially decorated and embellished for the occasion.

Another category of Chinese boat which may be reasonably well identified is the *lorcha*. Essentially a ship built in the European manner but Chinese rigged, the lorcha is first mentioned as a type in 1540. It is thought to have been introduced by the Portuguese and as a rare example of two-way technical trade with the Chinese the lugsail, not mentioned in Europe until 1650, may well have been a western adaptation of the Chinese rig.

Japanese junks are said to have changed very little since the sixteenth century when they were heavily influenced by the first contacts they had with the Portuguese and later with the Dutch and English. Their appearance was however more reminiscent of a Roman trader with a fine bow and high stem post and a sheet which rose to a full fat stern. The rig was even more Roman with a large pole mast setting a single squaresail nearly amidships and a smaller mast setting an artemon-like sail near the bow. The oddest thing to western eyes is the stern, which was broad and flat and provided with a wide opening which may extend half way down to the water. It is thought that this feature was originally used for working a single or double rudder and then was forced on builders by a curious shipping law. It was then retained as a very convenient entry port for craft lying stern-to at the quay.

Between the China Seas and the Mediterranean are literally hundreds of sailing communities which developed distinctive ship types of their own but were largely influenced either by Chinese or Arab vessels. Most of their history is lost but the ships which were sailing about half a century ago, probably represented fairly accurately the craft to be found in a particular area some hundreds of years before.

The Nile craft still represent a specialized version of the Arab craft and two principal types were the *gaiassa* and the *dahabia*. The former was a straightforward cargo carrying boat, redeemed by the most beautiful and graceful lateen rig. Gaiassas were rigged with one, two, or three masts depending on

Top left A modern day Portuguese boat with a single mast carrying a cargo of grass or reeds.

Top right A Chinese junk from Hong Kong.

Left Japanese Junks. These ships little changed since the 16th century, resemble a Roman trader in appearance.

Right A Baggala of the
type which can be found
between Ceylon and the
Maldive islands.

their size and the principal reason for such a lofty rig on workaday vessels was to catch the upper wind while sailing between high river banks. The dahabia was the pleasure version with a comfortable saloon aft and cabins for passengers and even a sundeck roof. For up river work with the wind, they carried a large sail on the mainmast and a small lateen on the mizzen. For down stream work the large sail was removed and the small mizzen set up in its place.

The *dhow* in its many guises was the work boat of the Red Sea and the Arab trading ship to East Africa, India, and even, it is said, as far afield as to Burma, Indonesia and China. Almost everywhere it went regularly the distinctive lateen sail was appreciated and adopted, usually with only minor local variations. The name dhow is not a generic term used by the Arabs themselves who identified their vessels more in terms of size, use, and where they were built.

Many of the exotic names are no more than the local word for boat

In fact a great many of the exotic names for boats are no more than a local word for boat, carried back as a technical term by western travellers.

The *baghla, baggara,* or *bagala,* or even *bugala,* was the main cargo carrying dhow and the name itself is said to mean mule, or load carrier. It was another type with an apparent resemblance to the caravel, with its long raking bow and long sheer rising aft with an aftcastle only. The rig was also similar with two lateen sails with the larger forward, but the sails were the Arab lateen which is quadrilateral compared with the triangular form of the Mediterranean lateen. There can be no doubt that either the early Portuguese or the Arabs were very heavily influenced by their early contacts, for the baggara shows many of the details which became common in sixteenth and seventeenth century western ships, including the highly decorated projecting stern transom and the lower hull finished with a curved planked tuck.

The *sambuk* was a somewhat similar dhow used mainly in the Red Sea and for voyaging to the ports north of Bombay, again with a long fine bow, flat floors, hard bilges and a long fine run aft, in this case to a flat transom. The booms, built in Kuwait from Malabar teak, had a very elongated stem post which was used to support a high raking bowsprit on which a jib was set in addition to two lateens. The *ghanja* was a three master with a very elongated poop, projecting well aft of the transom and possibly showing some Chinese influence. A dinghy was carried slung underneath the projection.

On the African coast the dhow was often given its local name of *gehazi* but this covered a wide range of sizes from small single masters, up to double masters, all of which might generally be categorised as baggaras. On the other side of the Red Sea a quite different hull shape influence shows in the *zaruks,* double enders of about 50 tons and 45 feet waterline, and the *badans,* which were somewhat similar except for the bows. The zaruk had an extremely heavily raked stem meeting the keel as much as a third of

Below left The Nile
craft represent a
specialized version of the
Arab craft. This
illustration shows a
dahabia, the pleasure
version of the gaiassa.

Below right A harbour
scene with junks in the
port of Calcutta India.

the length from the bow. The badan, on the other hand, had a near vertical bow with a vertical stem plank elongated forward, to make a clipper shaped cutwater. At the stern was an enormous barn door type rudder which was fixed straight fore and aft with a long deep·rudder working on the extreme end of it. Who can tell how such craft developed? It is tempting but unlikely to take some European credit for the handsome dhows and to let the more curious craft be a purely local product.

The zaruk was probably a straight descendent from the Arab *batelles,* principally used by the Joaseme pirates of the Persian Gulf. They were the terrors of sailing shipping in the area until they were put down, with great difficulty, by the united efforts of the Royal Navy and the East India Company. It was said of them that no vessel ever built could sail so close to the wind. In size up to 150 tons, they were rigged with a large lateen amidships, a small lateen aft, and balanced by a jib set on a bowsprit. In calms they were propelled by sweeps.

Batelles of a more respectable nature came from the Bombay area and were principally used for trade. They belonged mostly to rich merchants and were built of teak and fitted out with the best of everything, although they were apparently quite small – up to about fifty feet in length. They were used to import cotton and teak and it is mentioned that their open holds were covered with bamboo mats lined with soft mud and that this was an excellent method of keeping cargoes dry at sea.

Still in the same general area, the *kotia* of Cutch was a small baggara, carrying the usual two masted rig. A parrot beak at the stem head was a distinctive feature of the kotia which also had a rather heavy looking stern. Small boats appear generally to be labelled as mashwas around the Indian Ocean and in their smallest sizes were used as tenders aboard the larger dhows.

Although there is a superficial resemblance to the dhow, no western ship has ever been built with a hull form quite like that of the *pattamars* or *pattamachs* used from Bombay to the Coromandel coast north of Ceylon. They were remarkable for the manner in which the keel was heavily arched and used in conjunction with a heavily raked, deep stem to provide a sailing fin in the first third of the length of the hull. The lateen rig is well set forward to balance this forward lateral area, which must have given the pattamar a quite exceptional windward performance. The sterns were well rounded but they were in general open boats of no great size and used mainly for carrying rice and general cargoes.

In the middle of the last century the seaboats of the Maldive and Laccadive Islands were labelled as being quite grotesque and antique in their appearance, with a very distinctive aquiline bow. By the end of the century the islanders were reported to have developed some quite good boats. The most distinctive of them must have been the large trading ships running up to a hundred tons or so, apparently excellent seaboats, rather beamy, but with unexceptional form and rigged very much in the European style of four or five hundred years earlier.

Above *A Badjan Prahu with a Bugis Praku behind.*

The mainmast carried a large squaresail with one if not two square topsails set over it. The mizzen was a gaff sail, where the earlier ships would have used a lateen and the forward mast, steeply raking forward, carried a small square sail very like the Roman artemon.

Different yet again were the ships of Ceylon, of which the most striking were the *doni* or *dhoney*. These were the largest trading vessels of Ceylon

These many types of ship display almost every feature of Western sail

and were used for trade to all parts of the Indian archipeligo. They were usually about 65 feet in length and 20 feet in beam with a rather fine hull shape with a sweeping sheer. They were rigged with two lugsails, possibly showing more Chinese than Arab influence, and a jib set flying to the bowsprit end. To support this rig on the fine hull form they had to make use of outriggers. They were also interesting in construction for they were generally sewn together with the seams protected by a long batten pulled down over the seam caulking on the outside of the hull.

The Ganges 'country boat', also called a *budjerow* and sometimes just a *Bengalee* boat, was built up to about 60 feet in length and fitted with a single squaresail, with one or two topsails set over it, probably depending more on the standing of the owner than the need for sheer power. They were often used as pleasure vessels and sometimes were to be seen voyaging with a separate kitchen boat in attendance. They had high sterns and were full amidships and round bottomed, and were used almost exclusively for travelling on the Ganges. The principal work boat of the area was the *patile*, a large sailing barge with a single squaresail but with a particularly Indian style of rudder shaped like a flat spoon so as to be balanced to reduce steering loads. Such a rudder would also when put hard over form a quite effective brake, which would be of value in crowded river work. Equally interesting is the fact that they were clincher built, a construction which might be thought almost eccentric with nothing but carvel construction for thousands of miles in any direction.

The coasters that traded from Rangoon up and down the Burmese coast and to the Mergui Archipeligo off the coast of the Malay peninsular looked like the physical meeting point between the Chinese and the western influence in rig. Some of them were schooner rigged with a Chinese sail forward and a large gaff mainsail aft. They were mainly light weather craft, for the south west monsoon brings such strong winds and heavy seas that the trading vessels were laid up for the hard weather from June to about October. In the rest of the year they did not attempt a long voyage except with a fair monsoon and would seldom beat to windward except with a fair tide under them. The Malay east coast trader came in two distinct styles either looking like an American schooner with clipper bow, gaff main and foresail with topsails set over them and a full set of jibs and staysails over a long bowsprit, or else a very

similar hull could be seen with a full Chinese rig on it.

The *penjajap* was another east coast craft at the junction of east and west. It had a hull of rather European form, allied with a Chinese type double transom and driven by a two masted Chinese rig. The combination was not very happy and it is said that they made a practice of using bundles of bamboo lashed along under each gunwale, to add some much needed stability in anything like a breeze.

In the Gulf of Siam perhaps the most typical craft was the *rua pet*. Rua is the local word for boat and pet for duck, and the boat was so called from the resemblance of its nice fat rounded hull to that of a duck. The rua pet hull had a great deal in common with the seaworthy form produced this century for cruising yachts and with her two masted rig was above all an excellent seaboat. The *rua chalom* was a long shallow draughted boat, preferred by the Chinese and Chinese/Siamese for fishing. It had two side rudders of the most antique form, dating back to the first advances from the steering oar.

The Malay Archipeligo, stretching as it does from Sumatra, Java, Borneo, through the Celebes and the Moluccas to New Guinea and the Solomon Islands, is a marvellous area for seafaring, with its thousands of islands and inlets for shelter. It is not surprising that most of the local craft were small since there was no great economic or rough water reason for size. It is also unsurprising that quite different boat types were evolved and prime among those must be the *proa*, *prau*, or *prahu* (in fact the Malayan word for boat). The flying proas of the Ladrone Islands (now called the Marianas) in the north were among the swiftest and most ingenious vessels ever devised. Contrary to the practice of

Far left *Sailing praus, double-outrigger canoes on Sanur beach Bali.*

Left *A boat of the Batak tribe, North Sumatra on Lake Toba.*

Left *Double sailing canoes from Papua New Guinea. This tribe builds its houses in a shape similar to that of its boats, believing that their first ancestors came from the stars in such vessels. A spirit ancestor's head is carried on the bows.*

135

shipbuilders almost everywhere else in the world, the flying proa builders made their craft assymetrical. Not only were the two sides of the main hull of different shape but they were also fitted with just a single small outrigger. The remarkable feature was that when moving from one tack to the other it was the mast, sail and rudder which were turned and not the boat which merely started off again with the other end as bow. The ingenuity of this approach, coupled with the high power/weight ratio which could be achieved, gave quite exceptional speed and twenty knots was not thought to be remarkable for a forty footer in a good trade wind breeze.

Could the colonization of the Pacific have been made in these vessels?

The *corocora* was a curious looking vessel, mostly used by the Molucca islanders. It had a narrow hull with high stem and stern, something like a Viking ship but fitted with the most lofty long mat sail, which was set on a tripod mast. To give stability for this high rig they were fitted with one and sometimes two outriggers. In windless conditions a plank would be laid down over the outrigger beams and the crew sat out there to paddle. The *jellores* of Sumatra had a similar sail and were somewhat like the corocoras, although not quite so good looking.

The Pacific Islands were much more isolated during the centuries when the sailing ship developed and were much less influenced from outside. In most instances the islanders were also only interested in travel between islands of the group and were without any real pressures to go in for size and ocean trading. Some of the canoes they built were sixty or seventy feet long and they came in all types and sizes, with single or double outriggers. It seems quite credible that colonizing was done in such craft, for in such fertile areas there would be no need to take tools, equipment or food in any quantity on the passage.

There is of course, the mystery of how the islands of the Pacific were colonized in the first place and there are numerous theories of the origins of the various peoples. The voyages of Willis' 'Seven Little Sisters' and Heyerdahl's 'Kon Tiki' have done much to strengthen the belief that early immigration could well have originated in South America. Such voyages can only substantiate the likelihood of the theory being true and in the same way the study of information about earlier ships can only help to substantiate theories as to the origins and derivations of rigs and hulls. Many of the vessels mentioned in this chapter have already disappeared altogether and can no longer be studied in practice, but it is nice to think that there may be others which may linger in the odd harbours and waterways of the world or may still be met with when sailing the remoter seas.

Left Sailing boats from Bali. The distinctive outriggers used in this part of the world help to stabilize the vessels.

Chapter VIII
Twentieth century sail

This picture shows the sail training ship Malcolm Miller, sister ship to the Sir Winston Churchill.

When the industrial revolution changed the face of the earth it also changed the face of the sea. It was said at the time that never again would we ever see the clouds of white sails which had embellished the scene for centuries. The coming of the steam engine and the internal combustion engine had replaced the seven thousand year old era of sail, with tall funnels belching smoke. Very few people at the start of this century could possibly have envisaged the scene today when there are probably more

Right *The Vasa, built in 1628. She had a displacement of 1300 tons, a beam of 37 feet and a draught of 16 feet. She also had 12,378 square feet of sail. This drawing is by Nils Stodberg.*

Far right *The SS Constitution during her reconstruction. She is now preserved in her building port of Boston, Massachusetts. She was built in 1797 as part of a fleet of six ships which were to form the basis of the US navy.*

Centre *The stern of the Vasa, from a drawing by Gunner Olofsen. The height is 65 feet and she has double galleries. In the upper part there are two large windows for the captain, between which there is a device showing two corn sheaves held by Cherubs, which are a symbol of her name. There is also a national coat of arms supported by lions.*

Right *The Vasa was excavated in the summer of 1961. Her decks were housed in an aluminium construction. This has the advantage of allowing for regulation of humidity to assist in preserving these remains.*

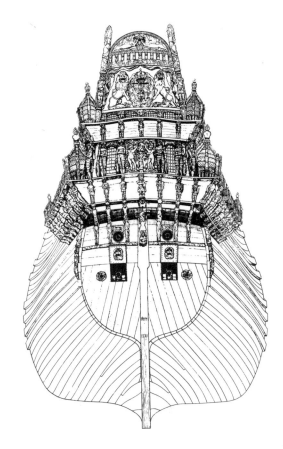

people in the world with actual practical experience under sail than ever before in history. As commercial sail faded, so began the day of the pleasure sailor and a surprising return to sail training for seamen bound for steamers. Another facet is the intense interest in the sailing ships of earlier generations. Relics are carefully dug out of bogs and painstakingly reconstructed and quite handsome sums of money are subscribed towards the preservation of notable sailing ships which have long since ended their commercial lives. Ships which were in fact of little interest in their day are often lovingly restored, even if otherwise fully documented, as if we cannot bear to lose a single extra specimen of the last of man's sailing heritage.

Many of the early relics are of great archaeological importance and it would not really be possible to be as certain of the details of early ships as we are without the physical presence in museums of such treasures as the ship from *Cheops'* pyramid, various remains from early Mediterranean shipwrecks, the *Nydam, Gokstad,* and *Oseberg* Viking ships, and the *Sutton Hoo* and *Graveney* remains. We now also have the *Bremen cog* in process of preservation to illuminate another dark period. Among the most impressive remains ever to have been brought up, as opposed to having been kept out of pride, is the ignominious wreck of the Swedish ship *Vasa*. Originally ordered by the King of Sweden in 1625 as part of his rapidly expanding fleet, this 230 foot by 38 foot three masted warship, displacing about 1,300 tons, keeled over and sank a few yards from the start of her maiden voyage in 1628. The disaster which drowned thirty of her crew was blamed on too fine a hull shape, which prevented the ballast being stowed low enough and on the lowest gun deck being too close to the waterline with the ports open when she heeled. Most of her main armament was salvaged at the time and she lay, probably thankfully forgotten by all concerned, until she was relocated and brought to the surface again in 1959. Now she is being most carefully looked after and scientifically treated to make her immortal as the sole representative of the many fine ships of the period.

The earliest existing ship which was not ever abandoned or taken out of service is *HMS Victory,*

The Victory, the oldest ship never to have been out of service

Nelson's flagship at Trafalgar and already an old ship at the time. Building of the Victory actually strated in 1759 at Chatham, to the design of Sir Thomas Slade, senior surveyor at that time to the Royal Navy. With a hull length of 226 feet, she compares with the *Vasa* in length but has the much greater beam and may have displaced as much as 4,000 tons in full commission. During her life she was extensively rebuilt to keep her up to date and in the last few years she has had considerable parts of her structure replaced to keep her sound. Victory lay afloat in Portsmouth harbour for a hundred years before, in 1922, she was moved permanently into the world's oldest graving dock and was restored to her Trafalgar appearance.

Next in order of date are the American super frigates the *Constellation* and the *Constitution,* both now preserved in their building ports of Baltimore and Boston respectively. Both were built in 1797 as part of a fleet of six ships which were to form the basis of the US navy. They are both about 204 feet long with 43 feet of beam and are 2,200 tons. The design is said to have been inspired by the French *razées,* three-deckers cut down to single deckers, to make strong and steady, but rather slow, frigates. The Americans fined the hull lines as well and added the magic dimension of speed. The hull design was said to have been a great influence on the early Baltimore clippers.

Other ships of many types built since those days have been preserved. The brig *Niagra* which lies hauled out in Pennsylvania as a museum ship was built in 1812 and is famous for her association with Admiral Perry and his flag embroidered with 'Don't give up the ship'. The frigate *Trincomalee* built in Bombay in 1817 lies in Portsmouth Harbour as the training ship *Foudroyant* and a near sister ship, the *Unicorn,* laid down in 1794 but not completed until 1824 is a museum ship at Dundee. The whaler *Charles W. Morgan,* built in 1841, a full rigged three master, is preserved as a museum ship at Mystic Harbour Connecticut. She is painted with gunports in her original style, for she was built when it was necessary to deter pirates, and is fitted with the heavy wooden boat davits which distinguished a whaler. The *Star of India,* preserved at San Diego, is an iron ship built on the Isle of Man in 1863 as the full rigged ship *Euterpe,* hull length 216 feet,

beam 29 feet, and used for a very varied life which included running emigrants to Australia and supplying the Alaskan canneries. The *Balclutha,* built in 1886 in Glasgow, has come to rest as a museum ship in San Francisco after starting out in general trade and also finishing on the Alaskan cannery run.

Perhaps the most renowned of all the sailing ships of this period which has been kept for our wonder and enjoyment is the *Cutty Sark.* Built in Scotland of composite construction she was originally a tea clipper but really became famous for her contests with the *Thermopylae* on the Australian wool run. She frequently made record voyages and is said to have reached a speed of seventeen knots on many occasions. Now she is preserved in dry dock at Greenwich, fully rigged and showing off her 224 feet of severe elegance.

Then we have the ships made famous by the Arctic and Antarctic explorers and which have been preserved rather as monuments for their feats. The oldest of these is probably the *Fram,* built in 1892 for the famous Arctic expeditions of the Norwegian polar explorer, Nansen, for whom she was built. She was also used by Amundsen when he went to the South Pole in 1911 and therefore has the distinction of having gone further north and further south than any other ship. Fram was built of wood by the famous designer and builder Colin Archer at Reykavik in an extremely strong manner so as to be able to withstand ice pressure when frozen in. She is 117 feet in length by 36 feet beam and rigged as a three masted topsail schooner, and is about 400 tons.

The Fram and the Discovery, heroes of Arctic and Antarctic exploration

In London, the 171 foot *Discovery* lies alongside the Embankment. She was built at Dundee in 1901 on the lines of the Dundee whaler, especially for the British Royal Antarctic expedition of the same year, commanded by Scott. She was also used by the Hudson's Bay Company and for running arms to Russia in the World War I. Since her final voyage to the Antarctic in 1928-31, she has been used as a training ship and museum.

Two other little ships commemorate the last great exploration of the earth – the final threading of the north-west passage round the north of Canada. Amundsen's little *Gjoa* of 50 tons now lies in San Francisco. Between 1903 and 1906 this converted fishing sloop, with seven men on board, persisted between freeze-up and freeze-up, sailing gradually westward until finally she reached the Pacific. It was not until 1940 that the passage was made again, this time by the 104 foot auxiliary schooner *St. Roch* belonging to the Royal Canadian Mounted Police which started a two year voyage eastwards to Halifax, returning westwards in 1944. She is now preserved in a special building in Vancouver.

Another phenomenon of the current fantastic interest in sailing ships of earlier times is the building and sailing of full sized replicas or reconstructions. Some, of course, have been built specifically for film work but many more serious attempts at

Right The bow of HMS Victory, Nelson's famous flagship. She is now preserved in Portsmouth harbour. She was an old ship when she entered service for him.

authenticity are based between archaeological interest and national or institutional pride in past glories. The Scandinavians have made several Viking ship replicas and one was rowed across the Atlantic to add to the evidence for the Norsemen having discovered America long before Columbus. The *Santa Maria* herself has been the subject of reconstruction attempts but these have been based largely on estimates of what a normal nao of the period would have been like, for instance, there are no technical details available. A replica of the *Golden Hind* was built at Appledore and launched in 1973, once again as the result of intensive research into ships of the period, rather than from any exact information about the Golden Hind herself. Fortunately, however, there remains a little basic guidance from the recorded dimensions of the dock the actual ship was preserved in until she fell to pieces. The new *Golden Hinde* (as they prefer to spell it) is to make the voyage to San Francisco where she will become both a memorial to Drake's landing in the vicinity and a tourist attraction.

A few years earlier Hinks of Appledore, who built the Golden Hinde replica, completed another antique type of vessel to celebrate the third centenary of the founding of the Hudson's Bay Company. The original *Nonsuch* was built at Wivenhoe, Essex, and crossed to North America to trade with the Indians in 1668. On her return King Charles II gave a charter to a group of merchants to trade with the Hudson's Bay area. The new Nonsuch, as close

as possible, of course, to the original but based on fairly flimsy details, is a fine little square rigged ketch of 53 feet in length and with a beam of 15 feet 6 inches.

Other ships associated with the early days of American history have also been the subject of conjectural reconstructions. Full sized vessels, representing the ships which the Virginia company despatched with settlers to Jamestown in the winter of 1607 are now moored in Jamestown. These represent the *Susan Constant*, recorded as being 100 tons burden, the *Godspeed*, 40 tons burden, and the *Discovery*, 20 tons burden. The two larger ships are said to have been colliers before they were bought for the Virginia run and the Discovery was said to have been a pinnace more suitable for the coastal trade. The Discovery was thought to have been used subsequently for survey work on the American coast. Also that it was her charts which were used by the *Mayflower* on her historic arrival in 1620.

A replica of the Mayflower was also built, in Brixham in 1956, and in 1957 sailed for a commemorative voyage under the command of Alan Villiers to arrive at Plymouth, Massachussetts, where she is now a museum ship. The reconstruction, again built with the minimum of facts to go on, had a length of hull of 106 feet and a beam of 25 feet.

It is probably fair to comment, that many of these reconstructed vessels, of the time before building plans were kept or even made, are not all that

Below The Fram at the ice barrier during the South Pole expedition of 1910-1912. She was built in 1892 for the famous Arctic explorations of the Norwegian polar explorer Nansen and used by Amundsen in the 1911 expedition.

Left The interior of the training ship Foudroyant at Portsmouth harbour. She was originally the frigate Trincomalee, built in Bombay in 1817.

Below The Foudroyant in dry dock.

satisfactory. The mere absence of facts allows all manner of other considerations to creep into their design and construction. Some, for instance, have had to look like the craft shown in a modern painted reconstruction of the scene. Most have had to be adapted to become satisfactory museums, which means that headroom between decks has had to be increased. Most of them have had to be fitted with engines and made to meet current shipping regulations. Some, therefore, present a slightly uneasy

The history of sail is the basis of all modern seafaring

appearance to the eye. The reconstructions of later ships, on the other hand, can be more exactly based on the preserved plans and although liberties have to be taken in some areas they have probably been more satisfactory. The *Bounty II,* built for a film company in 1960, looks for instance a proper handsome little ship although to accommodate the film cameras and the twin engines she is at 133 feet in length no less than 30 feet longer than the original Bounty from whose lines she was built.

The two masted 130 foot schooner *America* laid British yachting by the heels in the famous race round the Isle of Wight in 1851. Ever since, the extraordinary and monumental series of match races for the America's Cup has kept her name in the public glare. It is not surprising that a replica of this famous ship should have been built in 1967 by Goudy and Stevens as a private yacht for the president of a brewing concern. What is slightly surprising is that the lines from which the replica was built were supplied by the British Admiralty, who had continued their good old practice and taken the lines off the original. Even such an historic and well documented craft has had to be slightly changed for the copy. The sheer has been raised six inches to improve the accommodation, the masts are less well raked, and a quarter of her ballast is now fitted outside rather than inside as in the original.

Possibly the latest ship to be subject for reconstruction in this manner, is the famous schooner *Bluenose,* champion of the international fishermen's races between the USA and Canada. Bluenose was built in 1921 especially for these contests and was lost in 1946 while trading to the West Indies. *Bluenose II* was built in 1963, to the same plans, in the same yard and modified only to give her proper charter accommodation for passengers and of course the inevitable twin engines.

Training in sailing ship handling has always been advocated by some seamen, as the only way to get a proper knowledge of the sea, wind and tide. The basis of seafaring which underlies all the modern miracle hardware of machinery and electronics with which the modern mariner is equipped. The advocates of sail training fought something of a rearguard action until about the last twenty years or so when suddenly the picture changed. Now there are sailing ships being built all over the world especially for the job and the Sail Training Associa-

Far left above *A reproduction of Columbus' flagship, Santa Maria, under full sail.*

Far left below *RCMP schooner St Roch, built in 1928, was the first ship to navigate the North West passage from West to East and on completion of the return journey, to have made the voyages in both directions. She was a 300 ton ship and her captain was Staff Sergeant H A Larsen. She had a crew of eight and is now preserved in Vancouver Maritime Museum.*

Left *The Nonsuch under full sail, near Dawlish in Devon, on passage from Exeter to Brixham, on 21st August 1969. The original Nonsuch was built at Wivenhoe, Essex and crossed the Atlantic to North America to trade with the Indians in 1668.*

147

tion races are better supported every year.

Many of the maritime nations of course, never stopped training under sail and, for instance, the Russians are reputed to run a large fleet from the great four masted bark *Krusenstern* of about 2,000 tons displacement, to modest schooners built especially for the purpose. They also took over the *Cristofero Colombo* as war reparations from the Italians, leaving them with her sister ship the *Amerigo Vespucci*. These are very large sailing ships, whose dimensions bear comparison with those of the *Victory* with a length of 269 feet, a beam of 51 feet, and of 4,000 tons displacement, although perhaps more on the lines of a frigate than a three decker. They both carry a crew of about 450 of whom a third are cadets.

Also part of the post-war redistribution was the German 1,800 ton steel bark the *Horst Wessel*. It took over from the *Danmark* as the US Coast Guard school ship and was re-named *Eagle*. Other close sisters of the Eagle are the Russian *Tovaristsch*, the Portuguese *Sagres II* and the current *Georg Fock II* of the German navy. Another ex-German sailing ship still in use, although dating from the

Far left Uphams shipyard Brixham, where the Mayflower II was constructed in 1956. She was massively timbered in the old fashion.

Left A fishing Schooner champion of the North American fishing fleet.

Below The Mayflower set out from Plymouth harbour in 1620 with 102 pilgrims on board and a crew of 20.

World War I reparations is the Polish *Dar Pormorza* which after service in France was sold to Poland in 1929.

The Danes run a 210 foot full rigged steel ship, the *Danmark*, built in 1933, borrowed by the American Coast Guard during the last war, and a smaller ship, also full rigged, the *Georg Stage* of 134 feet. Both take about 80 cadets to sea, in addition to the normal crew and instructors. The Norwegians had the full rigged 198 foot *Sorlandet* built in 1927 and have the 205 foot full rigged ship *Christian Radich*. The former took about 85 cadets and the latter takes about 100. The *Sorlandet* was also the last sail training ship to be built without an engine, although she is now fitted with a diesel. Another of the large and impressive sail training ships is the Spanish *Juan Sebastian de Elcano*, named after Magellan's old mutineer who completed the first circumnavigation of the world. She was built in 1927 and is 289 feet long, 3,750 tons displacement and is square rigged only on the forward of her four masts, making her a four masted topsail schooner.

These and many more represent sailing ships which, despite their current value for sail training are substantially relics of the sailing ship past. Even the smaller Swedish schooners the *Gladan* and *Falkan* are basically typical examples of commercial craft, which either have already or are now disappearing. The first of the latest breed of ships designed especially to give the experience of ship sailing, rather than to provide part of a training leading to a lifetime's profession of the sea, are probably the little Canadian brigantines *St. Lawrence* and *Pathfinder*, built in 1953 and 1963 respectively. These 60 footers were designed by Francis MacLachlan for the Canadian Sea Cadet corps and take 22 and 30 officers and crew respectively to sea, at a time. They are based at or near Toronto and are used mainly on the Great Lakes.

Although the Sail Training Association is principally a British organisation and the Tall Ships races the brainchild of that Association, it was not until 1966 that Britain had a sail training ship of her own. The *Sir Winston Churchill* launched in that year was followed by a sister ship, the *Malcolm Miller*, in 1968. These two three masted topsail schooners are 135 footers with about 26 foot beam and carry six permanent crew and 40 boys or girls. Since then the British Sea Cadets have built a 76 foot brig, *Royalist*, to take about 32 to sea and the Outward Bound Association has built a three masted schooner, the *Captain Scott*. Many other organizations are currently building ships along the same lines, using expensive outfits and labour intensive gear deliberately, for the pleasure and instruction they give. Many other youth training organisations, notably the Ocean Youth Club, are building modern yachts for the same purpose, but these are much less specialised and much more akin to the private yachts to be seen all around.

When the steamship took over the technical leadership afloat from the clipper and when iron construction superseded wood, two seven millen-

Right *The Royalist, training ship of the Sea Cadets.*

nium old craft skills were concentrated perforce on the yachting industry. Here, with fierce competition for performance on the one hand and owners who appreciated a fine finish on the other, boatbuilding craftsmen developed standards to equal any of the master furniture joiners ashore, whose work is now so assiduously collected and so valuable. The yacht too developed along its own path. Whereas before a yacht was essentially a vessel of the day fitted out for private use, it now began to look for particularly high sailing performances. As races usually started and stopped off the clubhouse, the courses were usually triangular and windward performance the deciding factor. This is when the yacht started to develop its own rig. The gaff mainsail, which it had inherited from the old Revenue cutters and from fishing boats which liked to vary their trawling speed, gave way to the Bermudan rig. Then from that initial straightforward triangular mainsail the emphasis fell on the fore triangle. The profusion of jibs of the early craft, gave way to large and blinding genoa jibs for windward work and that curious balloon sail, the spinnaker, for downwind sailing. The spinnaker is best described as a sporting sail and possibly more than anything else, emphasizes the different approach that the commercial seamen had from their modern day successors, to the control of their sailing engines.

The yacht *Britannia* of King George V was one of the early examples of hull form designed for yacht use, rather than by taking any inherited value from the commercial past. Her spoon bow was thought ugly when she was launched but now is taken as a classic ideal of the yacht form. Her gaff rig was replaced during her lifetime with a full Bermuda main and the presence of the King afloat did as much to advance yachting as a dozen advances in rig. Her style was developed further in the big J boats which fought for the America's Cup, perhaps the most beautiful and the most impractical vessels ever to be seen under sail. The Bermudan rig has of course been used for sailing yachts of a size equivalent to the big sailing ships. The 214 foot, three masted staysail schooner *Creole*, built in 1927, and the 170 foot *Carita*, built in 1959, show pure yacht lines in their hulls and pure yacht rigs above them. They make a pair of the most beautiful ships ever to be seen afloat.

Now the sailing ship, which started the century as an anachronism, may well return as an answer to the energy crisis. Mr. Flettner with his rotor ships in the 1930s was too soon perhaps, but it does look as if the technology of yachts, which has been pursuing a different path from that of ships for almost a hundred years, may well find itself as the link between the sailing ships of yesterday and the sailing ships of tomorrow.

Above A model of the racing yacht Britannia.

Right Creole, owned by Stavros Niarchos, is the world's largest sailing yacht in commission. She is 190 feet in length and has over 17,000 square feet of sail.

Credits

Picture Research: Judith Harris

George W. Allan: 122/3
Antikensammlungen Museum/Weidenfeld & Nicholson: 26B
Antikvarisk-Topografiska Arkivet Stockholm: 41B
Ashmolean Museum: 46BR
Aspect: 43
Barnabys: 110TR
Bibliotheque Nationale/Weidenfeld & Nicholson: 53
Lorne Blair: 132/3; 134/5
Denise Bourbonnais: 28/9
British Museum: 64T
British Museum/Weidenfeld & Nicholson: 71
Peter Clayton: 22T; 22/3
Cooper-Bridgeman Library: 38/9; 64/5; 68/9; 74/5
Douglas Dickins: 134TL
C. M. Dixon: 36/7
Laurence Dunn: 120T; 149B
Edistudio: 32T
Editrice SAIE: 56
Mary Evans Picture Library: 73; 111
Fram Museum Oslo: 144
John Freeman: 64B; 72; 83; 93
Sonia Halliday: 34B; 57T
Robert Harding Associates: 136/7
P. D. Hawkes: Cover & 143
Michael Holford: 2/3; 4/5; 9T; 12T; 14/5; 18/9; 23TL; 26T; 30/1; 50/1; 70T; 99; 102/3; 107; 108; 112/3; 118/9
Alan Hutchison: 42/3
International Labour Office: 8/9; 131BR
Keystone: 8T
William McQuitty: 6/7
Mansell: 16/7; 20/1; 27; 33T; 44; 52; 57B; 63R; 68L; 77; 78; 78/9; 82; 86T; 87T; 98C; 104/5B;

109; 116/7; 124; 125TL; 126/7; 128TR
Mariners Museum Newport: 108/9; 114
Maritime Museum & Warship Wasa Stockholm: 140T; 140/1; 141TL
Mas: 84
Mondadoripress: 94L
Museum National Antiquities Stockholm: 40
National Maritime Museum Greenwich: 50T; 51T & C; 60/1; 76; 80/1; 89; 90/1; 92/3; 96/7; 116; 145 & end papers
National Maritime Museum Greenwich/Weidenfeld & Nicholson; 54/5; 67
Naval Station Washington: 100; 141TR
Ny Carlsberg Glyptoteck: 34T
Piazzale dell Corporazioni Ostia/G. Tomsich: 32B; 33B
Picturepoint: 47; 138/9; 150/1
Popperfoto: 63L; 104L; 131T; 7BL; 134/5B; 146T; 149T; 152B
Portuguese Tourist Office: 66; 126TL
Mauro Pucciarelli: Back Cover
Radio Times Hulton Picture Library: 24/5; 59; 69; 70/1; 98B; 101; 110B; 118
Rijksmuseum Amsterdam: 104/5T
Ronan Picture Library: 84/5; 125TR
Royal Canadian Geographical Society: 146B; 148
Royal Norwegian Embassy: 45T; 46BL
SS Great Britain Project: 120B
Science Museum London: 10/1; 12B; 46/7; 70BL; 86/7; 94/5; 98T; 106; 110TL; 152T
Uffizo Florence/Weidenfeld & Nicholson: 68R
Capt. A. Small/Hudson Bay Co.: 147
Staatsbibliothek Berlin: 41T
Statens Sjohistoriska Museum: 45C & B; 46BC
Weidenfeld & Nicholson: 35; 58; 125B
Ray Woodward/Blandford Press: 88/9
Zefa: 23TR